THE
DOCTOR

With all good wishes
for 1992
John, Sheila, Mark &
Anna

THE
DOCTOR

Just another year

DR BARRY BREWSTER & JEREMY MILLS

PHOTOGRAPHS BY
DAVID SECOMBE

BBC BOOKS

ACKNOWLEDGEMENTS

Thanks are due to the team which made the television series: Caroline Carter, Martyn Clift, Alex Hansen and James Moss during the filming, Dave Monk, Alan Lygo and Stefan Ronowicz with the editing, and Paul Hamann for his overall watchful eye and encouragement; to Linda Mallory for her help on the book; but mostly to the people of Settle and the surrounding area for their generous cooperation and involvement in the project, often during the most difficult times.

JEREMY MILLS

Published by BBC Books
a division of BBC Enterprises Limited
Woodlands, 80 Wood Lane, London W12 0TT

ISBN 0 563 36109 3

Design: Peartree Design Associates
Set in 11/13pt Old Style by
Butler & Tanner Ltd, Frome, Somerset
Printed and bound in Great Britain by
Butler & Tanner Ltd, Frome, Somerset
Jacket printed by Belmont Press Ltd, Northampton

PREFACE

THIS IS THE FIRST and worst book I have ever written. Despite this the book belongs entirely to my patients, for without them there is nothing to tell. My only concern is for them and I sincerely hope that I have not offended any single one of them by relating these affairs. If in some unrecognised way I have done so, then I am deeply sorry and beg their forgiveness.

I have discussed many of these matters with the patients concerned, and changed a name or two where it seemed appropriate. None of the events is fictitious, and when I regard these everyday parts of my life I appreciate that I am a most fortunate man.

I must record my respect, gratitude and admiration for the film crew of Alex, Caroline, James and Martyn; and to David for his remarkable photographs which so appropriately illustrate the mood of this book. Their tact and sympathetic behaviour won the respect of my patients. To Jeremy Mills I can but simply write thank you for his collaboration and encouragement – the pain of which I can still feel.

I am very grateful to my colleagues, my partners and their families, but particularly to my wife Scottie and my own family whom, in my selfish enthusiasm, I have ignored far too often. My only excuse, and I really have none, is that medicine is the most demanding and the cruellest mistress of them all.

BARRY BREWSTER
December 1990

I WAS DEALING with my last patient of the day over at the surgery when Annie phoned, saying she'd had a couple of whiskies, felt really low and wanted my advice. I've known Annie for all of my twenty-eight years in Settle, and she seldom asks for help, so I knew the problem must be serious. She lives on her own in an isolated bungalow on a farm some 5 miles from town. When I got there the reason for her melancholy soon became clear.

Over another small dram of whisky she explained that fifty-five years ago next Friday she and her husband had been married. For her this wedding anniversary will not be a happy occasion, but a sad reminder of happy days now long gone.

Her fifty-fifth anniversary will only serve to remind her how lonely and empty her life has become. Her husband Robert suffers from senile dementia and has to be cared for in a nursing home where Annie had been to see him today. He didn't recognise her at all, and hadn't been able to communicate in any way. Not the reaction you want from your partner of fifty-five years.

Although her family live close by, Annie often feels very much alone. I suspect her main emotion is not self-pity but anger – anger because no one has been able to help Robert. As we sat in her kitchen, stories of their courtship came flooding out with the tears which rolled down her cheeks. She told me how as a serving maid living at Grain House she'd come across Robert when she was cycling to Settle. The first time they met was under the railway bridge at Giggleswick station, and he asked her out. Evidently he was quite an athlete and was on his way to run at Wigglesworth Sports so he said in a matter-of-fact way that it would have to be the following night before they went out.

They met increasingly as the months passed, cycling to meet each other halfway between their respective employments. The romance started in the summer and they were married the following winter. The wedding was at eight o'clock in the morning at Giggleswick church; it was still dark as their wedding bells rang out. Then they went to Lancaster for the day and had a meal there. That was their honeymoon – 12 January, fifty-five years ago on Friday.

Now those early days of excitement are distant in years, but crystal clear in her mind, and she feels cheated of her expectations, almost as though she'd been tricked into a life which has let her down. Hardly surprising that she takes solace in a bottle's offerings on occasion, and I joined her in a glass as we sat and I listened.

Annie and Robert's years of hard work have not brought a comfortable retirement, but a lonely life which is little more than existence in her mind. The joys of youth gave way to the pressures of middle age and merged into the tribulations of old age, without time to appreciate what should have been their golden years of retirement.

So Annie was understandably a little bit sad tonight; very understandably.

AFTER SUPPER, my CD player was gently pumping Wagner's *Tristan und Isolde* into my soul when the harsh warbling tones of the phone broke through, and forced me back to reality.

'Doctor Brewster? It's Pat from Greenfoot. I wonder if you'd come and have a look at Millie. She's had a bit of a fall.'

Pat is care assistant at the Greenfoot sheltered accommodation for elderly people. One of the residents there, Millie, had been found in her bedroom unable to move. Apparently there was quite a lot of blood about and Pat hadn't wanted to lift her in case she'd fractured her leg. I told her I'd be down directly.

At Greenfoot, Pat was waiting for me. Pushing open the door of Millie's room, I saw her small body crowned with white hair, lying on the floor, her right leg resting in a pool of blood. Pat had been right in her description on the phone: it was difficult to see immediately how serious the trouble was.

'I'm sorry to be such a nuisance,' Millie murmured in a weak voice. It never ceases to amaze me how someone who is obviously in desperate need of help will apologise with great embarrassment for having to call the doctor out. We rarely receive a rude or unreasonable welcome when answering a call, and there is usually some guilt or other emotion to account for it if we do.

'We'll soon have you put together again, just like Humpty Dumpty,' I said gently as I made the initial examination. Millie smiled, and in a faint voice asked, 'Is that Dr Lewis?'

John Lewis, one of my partners, is her usual doctor, but I was on call tonight, so it was to me that Pat's call had been routed. 'Don't you recognise my lovely face?' I asked, pretending to be wounded.

She was clearly a little shocked. It must have been frightening and disorientating for her, stuck there on the floor awaiting help.

I made sure there was nothing broken, then we lifted Millie on to her bed and put a disposable paper towel under her damaged leg. There was a nasty gash across it where she had fallen, but, as tends to happen in these cases, the amount of blood appeared to indicate a worse injury than it actually was.

I laid out the instruments and cleaned the wound, chatting as I worked. Since she was John Lewis's patient, I knew little about her background, but as I injected some local anaesthetic around the wound she told me that she came from a farming family in Hellifield, and had one son who now worked for Henry Waddington, the provender merchants in Halton West. Her husband had been married before, and I think she said that she had gone to the farm as a housekeeper after his first wife's death. They were later married and had two sons but one of them had died when he was three days old. He'd died of convulsions after being 'born very weak'. Millie's voice became distant as she recalled the infant. 'He died on me sister's knee. He's in Hellifield churchyard now. They had a place specially for babies and children then.'

Some of the stories which simply trickle out when you're doing these jobs can be quite heartbreaking. When Millie was a young mother, the rate of perinatal mortality was very much higher than it is now, and it was simply expected that a few young babies would die. But that didn't lessen the grief for the mother, and Millie clearly would always remember her baby who died so long ago.

She went on to ask me how long I'd been in Settle. When I told her it was twenty-eight years, she asked if I remembered Dr Tony. I explained that I took over from him when he went to Canada. 'So that's where he went,' she said, as though it was the answer to a problem which had been troubling her, but just as if it was only yesterday he'd left, having popped out for a loaf of bread.

Every so often she would repeat how sorry she was to cause all this trouble to all these people.

When the stitching was complete we tucked her into her bed and left her to rest. On the way out Pat asked me if I'd heard any news about moving Betsy, who also has a room in Greenfoot. She's been a bit of a problem lately, being disruptive, and generally upsetting the other residents. It's a frightening element of old age that sometimes the physiological changes in the brain can turn a mild, lovable person into a disruptive personality in the latter days of their life. This was just one such case. I was able to tell Pat that we were hoping to have the poor lady admitted to the psychogeriatric unit at Airedale Hospital near Skipton, which will no doubt be a relief for everyone at Greenfoot.

I knew Betsy years ago when I used to stand in her kitchen and watch fascinated as she prepared lunch for her son Albert and husband Jack on a single-burner paraffin stove. I also knew that Betsy, who used to play the piano for me, would never be happy or content until she could join Albert, her mentally handicapped son, who died some ten years ago.

On my way home I stopped at the surgery to clean the instruments I'd used. All those adverts for washing powder are right: it can be a real problem removing blood from anything if it's left too long, so we always make a point of washing the instruments as soon as we've finished with them, ready to be sterilised the next morning by the nurses.

When I pulled into the drive, the house lights were out, and I could see that my wife Scottie had gone to bed. It was time to switch off from an emotionally draining evening and hope it would be a quiet night on call.

IF THE DAY OF JUDGEMENT is a Tuesday it will still be Market Day in Settle, for nothing but nothing will stop this happening. The bangs and clatters of the market traders erecting their stands drifted down the road from the ancient marketplace, and heralded the start of another hectic day as I left the house to walk to the surgery this morning.

Tuesdays are always busy in the surgery and there was no reason to expect this particular grey, wet and windy day to be any different. People come in from the many and various corners of our 300-square-mile patch to the market and often combine it with a trip to see us. In a community where car ownership is far from universal and public transport seems to be declining, this is more than just economy of time.

As I arrived at the surgery, 50 yards away from my house, I could hear the first telephone ringing. For fifteen years now we've run a 'phone-in' every weekday morning for half an hour from 8.30 a.m. We set up the phone-in system because we wanted patients to know they could call the surgery at a set time when they would be able to speak directly to their own doctor. It enables us to give results of tests or answer simple questions. This improves communication, saves the patient the time and trouble of having to come in to the surgery, and helps us keep up to date with the latest state of play in a particular illness. As a result of the phone call, we can decide to pay a visit to a particular patient, or ask them to make an appointment if necessary.

It seems to work alarmingly well. I say alarmingly because as the number of patients and partners has grown, so has the popularity of the phone-in. Requests for cholesterol results; advice on the baby's feeding; an X-ray result; 'Can you call in to collect the chocolate cake Mum's made for you'; an update on the call you made to a patient at four o'clock that morning; all these are dealt with routinely during the half hour.

The problem is that with only three incoming phone lines and five doctors there are inevitably some patients who are not able to get through. I'm beginning to wonder if the frustration of hearing the engaged tone may not be worse for some people than the problem about which they rang in the first place. We'll have to do something about the system soon before it becomes strangled by its own success.

The daily phone-in

There was additional pressure this morning from an unexpected source. Ten minutes into the cacophony of ringing bells, with four out of the five doctors – Eric, John, Clare and me – taking the usual continuous stream of calls, Bill Hall's chair was still empty while the list of calls from his patients was steadily growing. We had been working on the assumption that he was returning from a skiing holiday today, and had arranged the day's duties accordingly.

When Barbara, our practice manager, rang his home she discovered he had returned from his holiday, but had stopped off as planned in London to pick up some material for his MSc studies. The cock-up could be blamed squarely on a wall 'organiser' which hadn't been changed after the New Year. When we looked at it in the less hectic light of the afternoon, we discovered Bill's dates had been clearly marked on it, and showed him away until Thursday. Not an example of the good communication which I'm always talking about, but an excellent illustration of the way a simple omission can cause a lot of hassle.

The receptionists worked hard on the phone, and some forty minutes and several cooperative patients later most of Bill's afternoon appointments had been postponed.

That still left an extra morning surgery to be covered.

I have yet to discover many advantages in the government's White Paper on Health Service reforms, but this morning one did present itself. Eric had been scheduled to attend yet another bureaucratic meeting, so he was able to phone his apologies and look after Bill's surgery instead.

With one problem solved, another appeared. A van arrived carrying workmen to resurface part of our flat roof, a day earlier than arranged. Most people would be pleased to see any workman ahead of schedule, but in this case it just posed problems. The roof is over two of our examination rooms, and somehow I didn't think our patients would approve of a face peering through the skylight as they shared confidences with their examining doctor. So we had to rearrange things to get around that.

Added to everything else, it was also the first time we had the television cameras with us recording our every move. I gave up watching my language after the first few minutes of chaos, and hoped that not all my heartfelt expletives were reaching the microphone. If things continue the way they have started, I calculate this series of programmes will not reflect the practice I have striven to perfect for so long in a good light! Then I caught Barbara, our practice manager, sighing again, something she's taken to doing a lot in these days of excessive paperwork caused by the proposed changes in the Health Service.

She was looking at a growing pile of forms on her desk, and when she glanced up and saw me passing her door I could tell she was in a mood to pounce.

'You do realise,' she started, before I had time to even attempt retreat, 'that these forms you are so keen to complete have to be with the Family Practitioner Committee by the end of this week, or else you won't get paid for anything next year.'

The stern tone of her voice took me back to school days, to the warnings issued when an essay was due to be handed in the following day and it was clear that no work had yet been attempted.

This was yet another batch of forms to be completed in connection with the new GP Contract which is due to be implemented on 1 April – a date which not only seems singularly appropriate, but also looms nearer with alarming speed.

My teeth were firmly clenched again within moments as I read some of the questions asked on this particular form which are, quite frankly, outrageous.

'How do you intend to discharge your duties to your patients?' asks one. I gave Barbara my immediate and succinct reply to that. Fortunately she is a broad-minded and understanding lady. Hell's teeth! After twenty-eight years of what I hope may pass for dedication, building up a reasonable general practice, that particular question on this particular morning drove hard into my reserves of patience.

The true effects of the changes will not be felt for months, or even years, but I sincerely hope we will not view 1 April 1990 as the start of a decline in the family doctor service. Unless considerable adjustments are made I have no doubt that, sadly, this will be so.

HAVING SORTED OUT these minor problems and irritations at the surgery which contribute to making our lives far from dull, I made a quick diversion to the fish stall in the market. Screeching to a halt behind the stall, I pushed my head through a gap in the

awning and asked if I could have my pair of Manx kippers and some herring roe 'round the back', so to speak.

'You can have them backwards, frontwards, sideways or any bloody way you like as long as you pay for them!' came the jovial reply, forcing a laugh out of me, even in my black mood.

At 9.25 a.m., with kippers, herring roe and camera crew in the back of my car, and a list of calls in the front, I set off on the morning's round.

First call was to see a remarkable lady at Harden Bridge Hospital. Built as an isolation hospital in the days when the only way to stop the spread of fever, infections and consumption was to keep the sick apart from the rest of the community, Harden now houses up to thirty-two mainly geriatric patients. We share their care with our neighbouring practice at Bentham some 8 miles to the south-west. The hospital is due to close soon, and the patients will be transferred to Castleberg Hospital in Giggleswick. Another victim of cutbacks, or a sensible rationalisation of out-dated methods of community medicine? I suppose, to be fair, the place was built as an isolation hospital and is therefore, not surprisingly, rather out of the way!

This change has thrown up a number of interesting problems. For generations Castleberg has housed and cared for many mentally handicapped patients of all ages. My partner Eric Ward and I have been directly in charge of them for over twenty years, responsible only to a consultant in Bradford some 40 miles away.

Although it has undergone a programme of refurbishment, some people have already expressed a reluctance to go to Castleberg because of an understandable but unfounded prejudice against being put into what they regard as the old 'workhouse'. For years the people of Giggleswick and Settle have accepted residents of Castleberg as members of the community, and helped provide suitable work for them. Several mentally handicapped patients from Castleberg used to deliver papers or help clean up the market square, and many local people work in the hospital as nurses or cleaners.

Compare this with the 'Not in my back yard' attitude of many towns and villages when proposals for even a small unit for people with mental handicaps are submitted. Councillors shout, property owners perspire and alarmingly vociferous objections are made. Yes, deep are the roots of prejudice.

To cap everything, I heard this morning of a rumour circulating in the town that my wife Scottie and I have bought Harden Bridge for a sum which varies between a hundred and a million pounds, and are going to open it up as a residential home when we retire!

IN THE DAY ROOM at Harden Bridge I found Magdalene Ayres sitting with the other patients. I'm always impressed at how she manages to look smart despite the frailty brought on by her ninety-two years, and compounded by a recent fall. She's one of those people who has tremendous bearing and presence. I'm sure if she found herself on a route march through the Burmese jungle she would somehow pause at 4 p.m. precisely, fold away her sun brolly, adjust her large flowery hat and produce tea and cucumber sandwiches.

Magdalene is in Harden at the moment because as a result of her fall, she damaged her leg. I told her that I'd had the report from the X-ray which had shown up a hairline crack of her left femur. I tried to explain this to her using the analogy of a broken stick. A full fracture is like a stick which has been snapped in two, whereas a hairline crack is like a stick which has been bent just enough to split the wood without actually breaking it. She also has a problem with an avulsion fracture – a chip of bone which was pulled off by a ligament when she fell. This I likened to pulling a piece of seaweed off a rock, and taking with it a small chip of the rock.

Magdelene can still walk with aid of a Zimmer frame, and I asked her to demonstrate. She strode off purposefully and I had to explain to her about taking small steps, especially when she turns. Too many elderly patients fall this way. When they've been doing well, they race ahead, forgetting an underlying weakness.

From what I saw of Magdelene today she'll soon be out again and back home. She's making remarkable progress and I'm sure with patience and gentle exercise she'll mend well.

As I DROVE out to Clapham, the sun was shining and the hills looked fantastic. If I'd had more time I would have put the roof of my car down. There's nothing quite like driving in an open-top car on a sunny winter's day with the heater full on, a cap to keep the head warm and Wagner blasting out of the car cassette.

I drove past Clapham Woods where I used to go shooting at some of the highest flying pheasants I've ever seen. They would be so high up when they came over the woods that they looked more like sparrows.

In the village I made a routine call to see Jim and Doreen, who both have diabetes. Then it was back in the car to battle against the relentless tick of the clock. In general practice, time is of paramount importance, and it is essential to use what little we have efficiently.

This is not the cold efficiency of business, but a careful strategy designed to give as much time as possible to each patient, and increase the number of people you can see. If you choose your route carefully, for example, you can see several patients on the way to or from a specific call. This 'Look in' visit can be made with an easy attitude, as though you had the whole day to spend with that particular patient.

Time is important in surgery consultations too. Skilled doctors can learn and resolve far more in five or ten minutes than others in twice that time. Not only that, but with a skilled doctor, the patient can often feel far more satisfied, more informed and less anxious as he or she leaves the surgery.

I remember watching the chief 'sparks' on a Dutch freighter out in the Far East. His agile fingers caressed the radio's dials, continuously monitoring several frequencies at once, and tuning each to perfection with small tweaks in order to pick up the best information available in the shortest time. It's much the same for the doctor. It's important to monitor all the signals being given off by the patient, constantly looking for any non-verbal signs which can reveal more than simply what is being said. A sigh, a raised eyebrow or a white knuckle can often change the emphasis of a consultation and be the key to getting straight to the main cause of the problem.

In Austwick I parked my car on the village green by the Game Cock Inn. I always park there on a Tuesday, so that patients know I am about and available. This time I nipped into Ellen Holmes's house for coffee and communication. In her eighty-six years of happy mobility, Ellen has laid out bodies in most households in the village. I like to keep an eye on her now to make sure she's going on well herself, and she, in turn, keeps me in touch with what's going on in the village. 'Did you know Brian had a fall last night?' or 'I saw Mary out with her new baby. She's worried he's not feeding properly.'

On the whole as doctors we aren't privy to much of the local gossip, but these neighbourly snippets are always useful. They mean we can casually drop in and see someone who hasn't wanted to bother us, or let the health visitor know about an anxious mum. It's a great advantage of living in a community where people still know their neighbours and take an interest in each other. On my way out from Ellen I sometimes pop upstairs to the bathroom, where I'm always struck by a small leaded glass stand which carries a simple message, 'Along the way, take time to smell the flowers.' It serves as an apposite comment on my inevitable haste.

ON MY WAY BACK to surgery I called in to see Bryn. He's just back from hospital after some remarkable surgery to remove a cerebral tumour. When I arrived Wendy, one of our district nurses, was just about to dress the wound, a six-inch incision on the back of Bryn's head and neck. Such surgery never ceases to amaze me; the skills involved are quite fantastic. Encouragingly, the wound looked very clean, and Mr Ahmed's stitching wouldn't look out of place on a piece of exhibition embroidery.

It was cheering to see Bryn doing so remarkably well physically and mentally so soon after such a major operation. I'm convinced his rate of recovery is partly due to his philosophy, which is very positive. With these cases you really need to have the right attitude and state of mind. Bryn and his wife Ann certainly have that.

There was only one cause of puzzlement. In the scalp above his right ear he has two staples. What function they perform is a mystery to me. I offered the thought that they are the surgeon's trademark, equivalent to the wood carver who always places a small mouse somewhere on his work – an idea which appealed to Bryn whose hobby is joinery. I told him to ask Mr Ahmed about the significance of the staples next time he sees him.

Alongside my chair as I sit here writing is the three-legged stool Bryn made for me as a Christmas present. When he presented it to me he said that it was the traditional design for a milking stool. 'But in your case, Barry,' he added, 'I think a gin and tonic table would be a more appropriate name!'

Looking down now I can confirm it works perfectly for that purpose – a treasured possession which has pride of place alongside my favourite chair, and next to my CD player.

BACK AT THE SURGERY I passed John Lewis, one of my partners, and Scottie, who as well as being my wife is one of three practice nurses. They were in the casualty room sewing up a young lad who'd cut his hand. Scottie tells me he had a lucky escape. He's a farmhand who fell off a silo on to a tractor, but was able to stand up and walk away with only a gashed wrist. The smell was wonderful – just like being in the middle of a farmyard!

Scottie and John put an extra stitch or two in his hand because he would probably be back at work within the hour. Tough, some of these lads.

We do a lot of casualty work here. The nearest casualty unit is at Airedale Hospital, about 25 miles away, so it's a lot easier for people to come to us to get repaired. In spite of people like him arriving covered in muck from the farm, we get very little in the way of infection in the casualties we treat at the surgery. With good washing of wounds, and careful inspection and removal of foreign material our luck seems to hold quite well. It also has a lot to do with the fact that the bugs we encounter are not resistant to antibiotics, whereas many of the types found in hospitals are.

MY TUESDAY morning surgery was like many others, fully booked with two urgent extras: a consultant who kindly phoned to discuss a patient at some length, and another casualty. The latter fitted in to time which didn't exist. By cutting a few corners, unmercifully using our practice nurses and cursing a receptionist or two quite unjustifiably along the way, I was finished by 12.40 p.m., in time to see two drugs company reps before gulping lunch.

Afternoon surgery was fairly routine which, it's important to point out, doesn't equate to boring. In general practice we get a lot of people who come to us with a cough or cold and the danger is to think of these as unimportant. A question we always ask ourselves and often the patient directly is why have they come to see us at that particular moment. In reality the symptoms they present to us are often no more than a justification in their mind for seeing the doctor.

After thinking about the person, knowing the background

and taking into account their attitude, it often turns out that they want to talk to someone about a problem which is not the one they've presented. As the role of more traditional providers of counselling and support such as the church and, sadly, the family dwindles, we are finding that ours is increasing. It's an important idea for new doctors who come to train in general practice to grasp. In hospital they see illnesses which bring a person with them. We see people who may have some form of illness. So it's always vital to make sure that you discover what a patient has really come to see you for.

Occasionally consultations which start off with tales of bad backs or headaches soon move on to a request that the doctor write a letter to a holiday company informing them of the patient's incapacity to travel. On further gentle probing it's possible to uncover a reason why someone wants an excuse not to go on holiday – anything from a sudden fear of flying to an unknown foreign place, to some sudden social or family problem.

In other cases help is needed to reinforce a decision already made, usually a negative one such as not to move house or change job. This is often revealed by giveaway phrases such as, 'I won't take the new job if it's going to damage my health, doctor.' It's sometimes an attempt to have a decision taken out of their hands. That's not to say people are always trying to duck issues; sometimes they simply can't see a way through the problem, which in fact their subconscious has clearly already decided for them. A reinforcement of these semi-hidden feelings can help some individuals through a difficult time.

There are other cases where genuine physical symptoms can be caused by what most people think of as stress. So we have to be very careful not to fall into the trap of treating the symptoms instead of the cause. If we don't get to the root of what is causing the stress, it may remain completely unaffected, but the 'cure' might become addictive.

The big problem remains one of time. I like to think we will always attempt to get to the bottom of problems, but the more we have to become 'cost effective' the harder that will be to maintain.

Just writing about the patients in this afternoon's forty-five-minute surgery may illustrate this.

The visit of my first patients, a husband and wife, was clearly

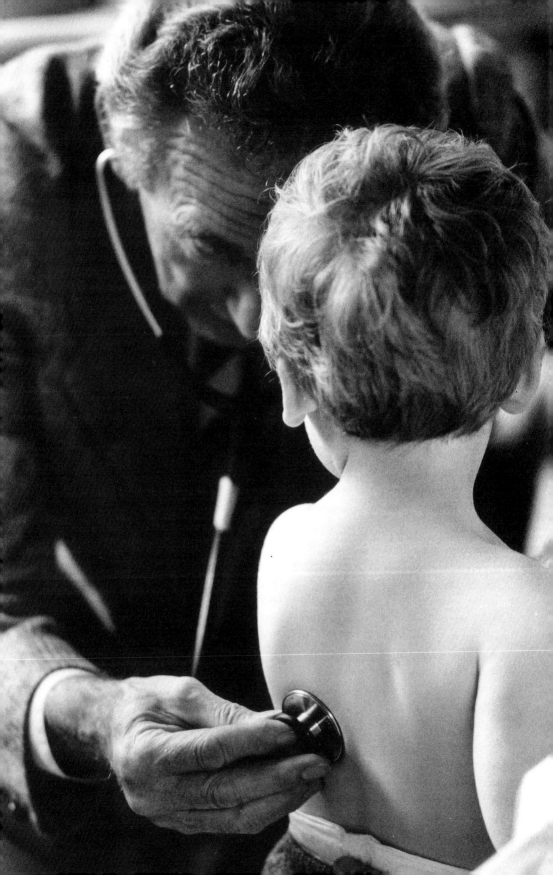

prompted by the consequences of a genuine serious illness, but what was uppermost in their minds at that moment was the way they felt they'd been handled.

She was clearly angry, while he was visibly upset and on the edge of tears. They'd just returned from the hospital where they'd been told that the cancer in one lung for which he'd been receiving treatment had spread to the other. This was obviously devastating news, made worse in their minds by a few thoughtless remarks from an obviously busy consultant. They'd come to me to receive reassurance. There wasn't much in the way of additional medical advice or explanation I could give them, but we spent a long time talking about quality of life, how they both felt about the situation they now found themselves in, and trying to address the whole business of attitude to the illness and the effect it would have on them.

It is possible to inform patients of serious illness without necessarily putting them into a state of shock. If they are deeply shocked, they become less able to understand what they are being told and to accept other information, and less able to ask questions and discuss their situation.

Had that consultant paused and considered how to couch the news he had to impart in gentle, but no less precise terms, then the couple who came to see me this afternoon might have started what is undoubtedly going to be a difficult time ahead in a more positive frame of mind. There's no doubt that the psychological state of patient and family can exert an enormous force on physical well-being, so poor communication is so frustrating. It means our own start line in the management of a family's problems is half a mile behind where it might have been, and the going a lot more difficult.

The next patient, a young lady I've seen before, wanted a repeat prescription for the contraceptive pill. After all the usual tests such as blood pressure and breast examination I asked her if she smoked. Sheepishly, looking down at her hands, she replied that she did. With the story of the previous patient firmly in mind I asked how many. She obviously knew what I was going to say, but when she told me about twenty a day I don't think she expected my outburst to be quite so vehement. 'If you want to ruin your life by buggering up your lungs then by all means carry on the way you are.' Although the content of the tirade was no surprise I suspect the style of delivery was. 'You can go on taking the pill for as long as you like and it will do you no harm on its own compared to the damage you're doing to yourself by smoking.' She was looking definitely uncomfortable by the time I finished, but had I achieved anything? When she left she promised to try and stop. Sadly, I doubt it will have made any difference at all.

After her came a woman I've known for years. Looking really pale and drawn, she asked for 'something for my nerves'. This almost classic statement is usually a signal for a fairly lengthy process of delving around in the patient's life to get to the root of the problem. In this case I was fairly sure I knew what lay behind the request, but it was only by knowing the background that I had the remotest chance of identifying the true problem correctly but swiftly. This lady is one of several people on my list at present who work for a local firm which has recently been under threat of closure. In an area where there are few job vacancies floating around it's hardly surprising to find people worried and upset while there's such a sword of Damocles hanging over their heads.

There were few options open to me in this situation, except to listen and possibly prescribe a mild drug to aid sleeping. I believe in this sort of case it is important for the patient to sleep so they can deal more effectively and logically with their problem in the daytime.

After a few more patients, mainly children who really had just coughs and colds, a woman came in to ask for the morning-after contraceptive pill, a misnomer for a start, since it can be used up to three days after intercourse. At first she put on a brave face and just said she and her husband had had an accident the previous night. I didn't dig for too much information, but as we were talking I gradually encouraged her to reveal the background. She explained that they'd been having problems in their marriage, but that last night after they'd made love he had announced he was going to leave her. Knowing the man involved he's a fool. He'll have to travel a long way to find another woman who will look after him so well – and if I see him I'll tell him so too. I listened and offered to see her again, asking her to be sure to make another appointment on the way out.

My last patient this afternoon really stumped me. I didn't know too much about her background since she's normally Bill

Hall's patient. She came in saying that she has been suffering from frequent bouts of nausea, constantly feeling tired and generally unwell. It turned out that her job involves her driving between Settle, London, Manchester and Basingstoke fairly regularly, and she had got to the point where she was quite often having to pull over to the hard shoulder to vomit. She explained that the attacks come on very suddenly, with hardly any warning, just a sudden sharp pain. She'd stopped drinking coffee which previously she'd enjoyed in large quantities, and instead had a craving for fizzy drinks. Although she'd not been eating she hadn't lost any weight, in fact she said if anything she'd put some on. I made sure she'd weighed herself on the same set of scales, which she had, ruling out a simple discrepancy between different machines. She'd also not been sleeping at all well.

She felt it might have been side-effects of the contraceptive pill, so had decided to come off it and sensibly had been to see Clare, our lady partner, to talk about alternative methods of contraception. Her periods and water works had been fine so there were no obvious solutions there.

After talking to her for quite a while it seemed the key to the problem was her job. The amount of driving she has been doing as a sales rep is obviously getting her down, and I was glad to hear that she's about to change her job, and move to a new flat in London which she said will also cut down the amount of driving the does. Being on the road from five o'clock in the morning to ten o'clock at night can't be good for anyone.

To be on the safe side I took some blood to be sent away for tests, and explained that it looked unlikely that we'd be able to work any miracles there and then. I will be very interested to see what, if anything, those results reveal. I must remember to ask Bill about the outcome.

So IN ONE FAIRLY brief surgery, cases which might at first sight have appeared to be mundane or at least straightforward, demanded time to listen, some investigation and sometimes careful suggestion or advice.

Overleaf: Time to listen

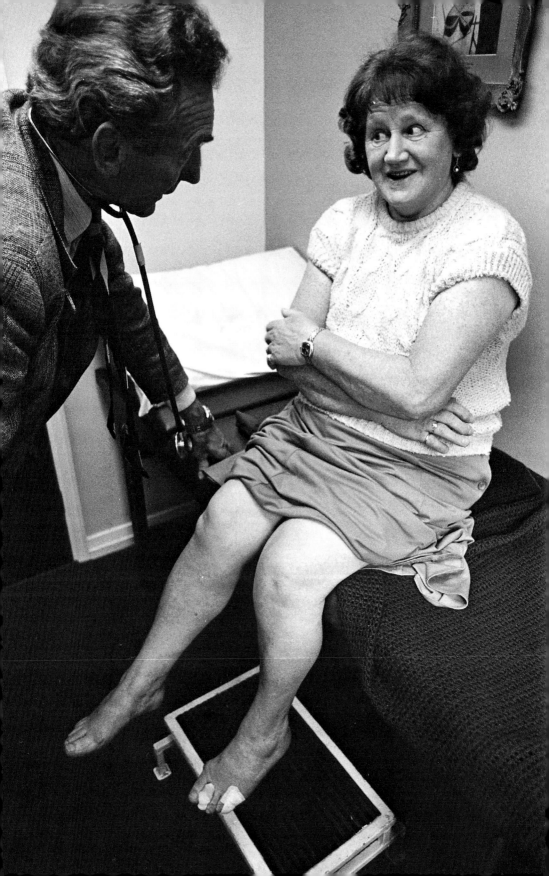

WEDNESDAY

10

JANUARY

TWO CONSECUTIVE CALLS on my round this morning provide an example of the diversity which continues to be one of the main fascinations of the job.

First stop was Langcliffe Hall. As I drove through the high double gates and parked in the large gritted forecourt this morning I thought of the times I used to go up there to see my old friend Michael Dawson, who sadly died some twelve years ago.

Michael occasionally asked me to go grouse shooting at Rough Close, up on the moors adjacent to Pen-y-ghent Hill. Very grand affairs these were – with splendid luncheon parties at shooting huts which were split in two: one side for the beaters, the other for the gentlemen.

This morning the Hall's huge studded front door swung open revealing the present owner, Michael's nephew Robert, with his black labrador, Sam. He led me up the sweeping staircase, past the beautiful stained glass window which dominates one of the landings and into his wife Betsy's bedroom. She lay in her four-poster bed looking a bit poorly and feverish, but it transpired with nothing more serious than the after-effects of a virus.

Having given her the all clear we climbed yet more stairs lined with oil paintings to the top of the house and the nursery. In the warm room Francesca lay in bed guarded by an enormous teddy bear. Fortunately she was also well on the road to re-covery. After a brief chat in the flagstoned hallway I crunched my way back across the courtyard to the car, catching a glimpse of Francesca waving goodbye to me from her bedroom high in the house.

Next to Willie Morphet, a farmer in his tenth decade. He has a degree of heart failure and some hypertension, as well as occasional bouts of angina. He regards all his symptoms as a damned inconvenience, so it went down very badly when he fell and broke his right forearm about eight weeks ago.

It had taken a great deal of persuading to even get him to hospital to have it X-rayed. 'It'll mend on t'own,' he kept saying. In a way, of course, he was right. All we could do was help it set as quickly and correctly as possible.

So we persuaded Willie to have it seen to and it was put in plaster. This did not suit him one bit because it interfered with his life, in particular his farming, and he moaned that it made it almost impossible to drive his battered Landrover around his farm. John Booth, his neighbour, commented that this latest injury wouldn't make much difference to his driving anyway.

Willie's a real old-style farmer, although he only has a few sheep to tend to now. Up until only a few months ago a neighbouring farmer on the other side of the valley used to say that he set his watch by Willie's morning activities. At ten past six every day he would look out of his farm kitchen window and see Willie feeding his beasts.

After the statutory minimum six weeks in plaster Willie was off to the hospital to get shot of the impediment. However, in the last couple of days he's been complaining that his arm is hurting. Paul, our physiotherapist, has been seeing him regularly and told me this morning that the arm was getting very hot, and I had little doubt that the pain would be associated with his overuse of the resolving fracture, quite some feat in a man of ninety-two years. He may even have an infection around the site of the break.

Just outside Wigglesworth I drove off the main road along the track which leads to the old grey granite farmhouse, where structurally nothing has really changed externally or internally for years. Once full of the sounds of a lively family, it now echoes only to Willie's solitary life. His Landrover was parked outside the green back door, while inside the large farm kitchen the single overhead bulb maintained the gloom of this stormy day. Willie was sitting by the range wearing an old coat tied around the waist with baler twine, reading the newspaper.

As I helped him take his coat off I asked how his arm and shoulder were. He didn't seem to be suffering any pain, but he's a tough old bird and I'm not sure he would show any signs even if he were. As I felt the rest of his arm I asked what he'd been up to yesterday. 'Well, just going round the sheep and giving them a bit of hay or something,' he mumbled, watching my hands feel around his arm.

For someone who has spent a lifetime manhandling animals and lugging feed around a farm Willie is very slight in build, almost gaunt. Comparing the damaged arm with the other sparrow-like limb it was clear that it was definitely swollen and warm.

Robert at Langcliffe Hall

When I made him squeeze my fingers his grip was quite weak, and he actually admitted the movement hurt him slightly in his bad arm, which probably means it's quite painful. He certainly flinched when I squeezed the damaged area. At least, he told me, it isn't keeping him awake at night, which in his case means bed by 6.30 every evening. A typical farmer's attitude that – no point in being awake during the dark hours unless there's good reason.

There was really no other option than to have his arm X-rayed again and for him to see my good friend John Cape, one of the orthopaedic surgeons. Willie grudgingly agreed it was probably the best thing, and said that he'd get his neighbour John Booth to take him down.

John and his wife Freda are extraordinarily good to the old boy. They're not related in any way but treat him like one of their family and are very thoughtful about generally keeping an eye out for him, giving me the nod if they think I ought to call and see him. It was typical of Willie to assume they'd drive him to the hospital, though I'm sure they will without question.

On my way out I called next door at their bungalow to tell them what was up, but as there was no one at home I left a note on the kitchen table to ask John to give me a call during the phone-in tomorrow. I was just putting the salt-cellar on top of the piece of paper when I heard Willie's Landrover roaring off down the lane. The old bugger couldn't bear to be sat still for another minute, painful arm or not.

I'VE KNOWN SEVERAL resilient farmers like Willie over the years, with high pain thresholds.

At 7.30 one wet winter's Sunday morning about fifteen years ago, just as the light was lifting, the phone rang. It was still dark and as I lay in the warmth of the bed listening to the steady drip of rain falling off the roof, I remember hoping it would not be a call-out.

It was a chap ringing from a village phone box some 5 miles to our north. Having identified himself he explained the reason for his call.

'Eh, Doctor, it's me brother. He's not so well.'

'Oh aye, what's up with him?' I asked, pulling the blankets further up around me.

'He says he's got a pain down below and he's not so good.'

Taking my cue from the lack of urgency in the voice I wriggled a few more inches under the covers. 'Oh yes? Where does he live?'

He described the farm which was some 9 miles further up the dale from the phone box. I asked when he'd last seen him, thinking it would have been earlier that morning or at least the night before.

'Oh about a week ago. He said he had a pain then.'

I couldn't quite get the time scale clear in my mind. 'So why are you phoning me now?' I asked, hoping to shed some light on the matter.

'Well I was just passing by the phone box and I thought I'd better ring you,' he replied, in an unconcerned tone, much as he might have done when remembering to pass on someone's regards.

I can only imagine he hadn't called before because he hadn't happened to be near a phone.

I don't know why, but the hairs on the back of my neck went up in a premonitory warning and something told me to get myself out there. The alluring warmth of the bed was soon forgotten as I drove out into the grey dawn of sleet and bitter cold. I got to the old, long, low farm and left the car up on the road because the drive looked a bit treacherous.

There was no sign of life, so I entered without waiting to be invited. The front door opened with the kind of creak you only expect to hear in ancient black-and-white horror films.

Inside, the enormous farm kitchen was so big I wondered how the ceiling kept up. Through the combined gloomy efforts of the dawn light and the small old-fashioned windows I could see the place was fairly shambolic. A rocking chair and few stools grouped around a big table in the middle of the blue slate floor; an old Aga which at least gave the place some warmth; and walls devoid of anything except a nail with an animal halter hanging off it.

I called out but there was no reply. I ventured further, beginning to conjure up pictures in my imagination of what awaited me, and not relishing the prospect.

Across the kitchen was another door which also performed its best audition for the Hammer House of Horror. Through this I found the passage-way, its half light in turn revealing the staircase in even more gloom.

I called again. The silence continued. Upstairs I could see another door, this time ajar. I looked in and just about made out a big bed covered in some rather grey white sheets. Amongst those grey white sheets on an equally grey white pillow was a slightly paler grey white face. An eye opened and looked at me.

'Hello, Vernon. What's the problem?'

'Well, I've a pain down below,' he replied in his deep Dales voice. 'It's one of me stones.'

'How long have you had it?' I asked, moving across to the bed.

'Oh, a couple of weeks.' He looked diffident, almost ashamed.

Not knowing what to expect, I pulled back the grubby sheets – to reveal a congealed mass of blood around his scrotum.

'Now then, Vernon, what have you been doing?'

'Well the pain was getting terrible a few days ago.'

I thought back to his brother's tale of his visit a week before.

'What did you do?'

'Well it was hurting something terrible and it were so bad by the evening I cut it off.' This was said very matter-of-factly.

'What do you mean, the stone that was hurting?'

'Aye.'

There wasn't a great deal I could say except, 'That's interesting, Vernon.' Taking in the full implications of this Do-It-Yourself orchidectomy or unilateral castration, I took my torch out of my bag and examined the area. I had already switched on the bedroom light, but 40 watts doesn't exactly floodlight a large grey farm bedroom. Seen for the first time in a decent light the wound was hairy, metaphorically and literally. I elevated one part of the offending mass and there was a trickle of fresh blood. Not wanting to disturb anything else I didn't probe too far and decided not to examine the precise location of the haemorrhage any further at that stage. I checked Vernon's blood pressure which was surprisingly satisfactory, his heart rhythm was regular, and other parameters were not too bad either.

I was amazed that although there was a mucky mass of clotted blood with bits of skin, and the surgery was by now some four days old, there was no apparent infection and no fever. A somewhat puzzling state of affairs.

'Well, Vernon, what did you use?'

'Oh, me penknife.'

I couldn't think of anything to say but 'I see.' I wasn't sure if I wanted to know any more, but decided to ask if by any chance he'd cleaned the knife first.

'Aye.' This gave me cause for hope, thinking he might at least have put it over a flame or washed it in disinfectant.

'Oh aye,' he continued. 'I wiped it with me handkerchief.'

I looked around at the state of the sheets and remembered the unwashed cutlery and crockery on the kitchen table downstairs. If his handkerchief was like the other possessions I could see it was hardly likely to promote the cause of aseptic surgery.

But whatever else there was no infection. Although looking at the results of the home surgery it was hardly surprising to hear Vernon admit that things were a little uncomfortable down there, but at least less painful than they had been.

The other aspect of the affair which did surprise me was the apparent lack of blood on the sheets, so I continued my quest for the truth.

'Vernon, you've obviously bled a bit, but I can't see very much around.'

'Oh no,' he replied, 'I bled a bit at the time, but I tied it off.'

'You tied it off?'

'Oh aye,' he replied; 'used me boot lace real quick.'

I glanced down at his boots lying under the bed, one minus its lace, which did nothing to alter my opinion that this had not been an aseptic procedure. Somewhere in amongst the clotted blood was a mud-covered bootlace which I certainly wasn't going to search for at that particular moment.

I thought it was about time I had a look at the offending piece of excised tissue. At least I would be able to hand it over to the pathology laboratory for analysis. This would reveal the cause of the patient's initial pain which had compelled such drastic action, and would help direct further treatment. 'Vernon,' I said, thinking myself to be in safe territory, 'what did you actually do with the stone you cut off?'

'Oh, I fired it?!'

I raised my eyebrows questioningly.

'Aye, I dropped it into the Aga.'

So the pathological evidence of the disease had gone out the window, or at least into the fire.

There wasn't much more to say. I looked at the injury, then at the patient. 'Vernon, you haven't strayed too far, have you, in the last few days?'

'Oh no, I haven't been so very far. Only out in the yard to feed the hens and out to the odd beast in the shippen.'

It was pretty clear he had to be got into hospital and tidied up, so I went to the nearest farm, where I knew the telephone was sited in the passageway away from the kitchen and so my conversation couldn't be overheard. I phoned my friend Dennis Shaw, a surgeon at Airedale Hospital. He happened to be at home that Sunday morning and I told him the story.

'The man's mad' was the only response from the other end of the line as the story drew to a close. I said I didn't think so; he was simply doing what he thought he ought to. After all, he'd done it to a few hundred lambs in his time, if for a different reason, and he was taking what he saw as a fairly logical step.

Dennis said he'd go in and be ready to meet the patient in the hospital in a couple of hours, as soon as the ambulance arrived. I think the idea of seeing this unusual injury and the prospect of discovering the bootlace intrigued him.

But he made one condition. He would tidy Vernon up if I agreed to get him to see a psychiatrist. I was glad to accept this part of the bargain, knowing my good friend Pat O'Brien, who is a great whole-person psychiatrist, would be comprehensive in his approach to Vernon.

In due time he was tidied up, given a little blood, and eventually saw Pat. The psychiatric consultation revealed that the patient was a great racing man, who marked up his paper very well every day, followed his football and in all respects was pretty normal. Dennis, the surgeon, accepted this with a wry smile, content in the knowledge that his patient was safe and apparently sane.

Vernon moved away a few years later and as far as I know is still living happily ever after.

THURSDAY 11 JANUARY

I'VE BEEN WONDERING lately if we are all destined to disappear under the mountain of paperwork. It's almost as if there's a determined effort by our Lords and Masters to make us spend so much of our day filling forms connected with the new Government changes in the Health Service that we won't have any time left to waste money on treating people!

At around 7.30 this evening I was in my consulting room trying not to get too frustrated and annoyed by yet more forms, and just wondering whether to pack up and go home for a gin and tonic when Donald and Shirley arrived at the surgery.

Donald was holding his chest, complaining of strong, dull pains which made it hard to breathe. He said it was all he could do to stop himself doubling up in an attempt to ease them.

His understandable and obvious concern was that the pain was associated with his heart. As I examined him I thought it was probably not a coronary thrombosis, but more likely to be angina – a sort of cramp of the heart muscle – so I gave him a drug which dilates the coronary arteries.

I felt there was something troubling him on top of the anxiety about the pain, and while we were sitting waiting for the drug to take effect, Shirley explained that indeed there was. Donald had just that afternoon heard that he was to lose his job, which could well have caused enough stress to trigger an anginal attack.

At this moment the phone rang. It was a very distressed mum with a screaming three-week-old baby boy. Having a wife who is a practice nurse has its advantages for me, and disadvantages for Scottie. I phoned home and asked her to pop across to the surgery to do an electrocardiogram on Donald, my angina man, who by this time was considerably better. Meantime I whizzed off to see the baby. On my way down the surgery passage I heard the nervous jangle of Shirley's keys echoing around the empty waiting room, and paused to reassure her.

FIFTEEN MINUTES later I was back in the surgery, having reassured the mother of the crying baby that he was not *in extremis*. The ECG complete, Scottie returned home to finish making our supper.

Looking at the ECG print-out, all seemed normal. Donald was much better and I was able to tell them both that I didn't think any heart damage had actually occurred. However, there were still some straws in the wind that had me hesitating about this patient. The hairs on the back of my neck were standing on end in warning.

I asked Donald and Shirley to wait a minute and went back to my desk where the ECG print-out lay. Looking at it again closely I could still see no obvious signs of cardiac pathology, no indication of any interference with the normal heart muscle activity, or the supply of blood to the heart. Donald had also responded to the drug designed to reduce anginal pain which indicated we might have been on the right lines there.

Yet the way he had described his pain when he arrived smelt a little of a dissecting aneurysm of the aorta. In this condition the various layers which make up the wall of the main artery from the heart are separated by blood which leaks between them. Something niggled and I'm a great believer in relying on instinct in these matters, so I decided to send him into hospital where he could be monitored more consistently.

It's always difficult to tell someone you're going to send them in. The last effect you want is an increase in the stress they feel, which in turn could make them even worse.

I explained that the ECG looked good, blood pressure was good, but since the pains had started a couple of days ago I felt I'd like to get him into hospital to be on the safe side. I explained by the analogy that we could probably drive the 16 miles from here to Skipton without seatbelts and get away with it, but it's obviously more prudent to wear them. In just the same way it would be safer to get Donald in where he could be monitored more carefully. I told them I'd get the ambulance to come down in a few minutes and take him in.

They both looked crestfallen at this news. Shirley asked if she couldn't take him by car. I was pretty sure there was nothing major wrong with Donald, but if he did have another attack on his way to hospital the ambulance lads could cope with the situation.

As I write this diary tonight, Thursday, 11 January 1990, the television news informs me the ambulance dispute is intensifying all over the country. Yet our lads are still working pretty well normally.

I was asking them earlier how they feel about the industrial action being taken by the unions. It's clear that they are in

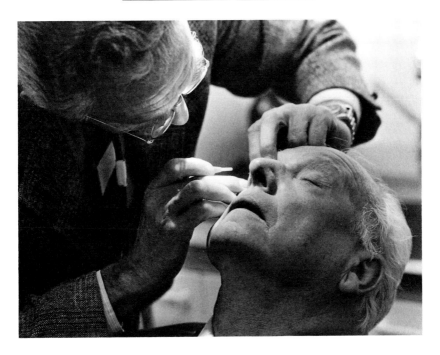

agreement with their unions' aims, but they also have a deep sense of loyalty to their community, to the extent that they feel it would be impossible for them to take action and refuse to help people. Only a few months back, for example, they'd appealed for several thousand pounds for a piece of equipment, a defibrillator, for their ambulance and it had been raised in a matter of days. In a small community like ours that's the kind of support you get. How, they were saying, could they subsequently turn around and tell those same people they were going on strike?

The two lads on the 'bus' tonight knew Shirley and Donald, and I heard Pete the attendant say to Shirley in his broad Yorkshire accent, 'You goin' 'ome to Janet's, then?'

She nodded affirmation.

'Aye well, take yer time. You'll probably catch us up anyhow, the way he drives.' These few words of jest helped ease the tension and made the impending hospitalisation less daunting.

THE AMBULANCE drove off into the night, taking Donald to be well looked after. I'll be interested to know what they discover with all their hardware at Airedale.

WEDNESDAY 31 JANUARY ISABEL CAN HAVE HER off days, but is remarkable in the way she accepts her painful disability and still finds the courage to laugh. I've known her all my practising life, and I remember her when she ran the farm at Tems House in Giggleswick almost single-handed. I used to see her in the shippen milking the cows, then brushing and cleaning out after their departure. On my way to see her this morning I stopped at Lamberts', the printers in the town, to pick up the key from her son Alistair. He's having another one cut to make it easier for me to call on his mother whenever I need to, without having to worry about getting in.

For three years, Isabel has been receiving treatment from Dr Dodds, our rheumatologist, for a dreadful combination of rheumatoid and osteo-arthritis. The pain she's subjected to now is quite gross and has become so bad she can hardly move without superhuman effort. Dr Dodds has done everything possible in terms of medication, but the time has come for surgery and a

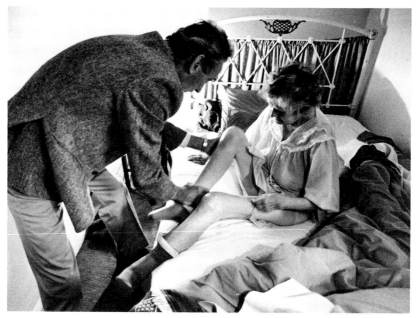

Isabel

right knee replacement. For Isabel, the way she is forced to run her life, depending on her son so much, is almost as difficult to cope with in psychological terms as the physical pain from the deformed joints. Despite this she has retained a great deal of dignity.

I called out as I climbed the open wooden stairs to her bedroom. I was sure she'd be in there; she's not really been able to move far from her bed for quite some time now. Her cats scurried about my feet as I climbed over piles of clothes which lay about her room. I found her perched on the edge of the bed almost weeping from a mixture of pain and frustration – the frustration from the fact that it was already mid-morning and she was barely half dressed.

'I'm so sorry about the state of the place, Doctor,' she said, running her crippled hand through her tousled hair. 'I'm stuck here. I can't get any further.'

Looking at her knees, hands and wrists it was easy to see why. Her hands are deformed and flexed by the rheumatoid arthritis that has so viciously attacked her. The knees held in flexion with wasting of the muscles above and below the joint show the typical rounded globe appearance. Isabel's sheer pain, so easily recognised by the eye, was most awfully appreciated by the ear when I helped her to stand. In the quiet of the bedroom, with only the ticking of a bedside clock and the cats toying with a paper bag in the corner, the noise caused by the friction of bone on bone was terrible to hear. The only comparable sound I've heard is the creak of the rigging in an old sailing ship, where wooden pegs groan as they rub against wooden blocks under the strain of huge sails. The clock's tick was lost against the noise.

She sank back on the bed with an agonised moan, and it took several seconds for her to recover from the pain and effort. Then, almost on the point of tears, she suddenly hit her hand on the bed and sighed, 'I can't take much more of this. It's been put off twice now, and I don't know how much longer I can go on.'

It is true that Isabel's operation has been postponed twice. The reasons for this are several. A surgeon only has so much theatre time and the demands on this time increase with new technology, the rise in emergency surgery, and longer life expectancy. As each road accident demanding immediate attention is admitted, or a chronic orthopaedic case becomes acute, so the cold surgery queue in which Isabel sits so painfully is lengthened.

I knew one of Isabel's main frustrations resulted from her fear of not being back home and up on her feet in time for her daughter's return from New Zealand at Easter. Typically though, when I told her I was due to see David Beard, the orthopaedic surgeon, within a couple of hours at the hospital when I'd do my best to make sure the operation wasn't delayed yet again, she sighed, saying she realised other people have families too and didn't want any favouritism. From a lady in her state that's a pretty brave and selfless attitude.

I left Isabel, promising to call in tomorrow to keep her in touch with developments. I'm sure she was in a slightly more positive frame of mind, at least happier in the knowledge we were doing all we could to make the system work for her.

My visit to the hospital was provoked by yet another ludicrous requirement of the new GP contract. We have to attend school for five sessions, signing in like children when we arrive to prove we've attended. This is in order to retain the right to perform minor surgery in the practice, or, more to the point, claim for doing it.

By coincidence it was David Beard's turn to be teacher today. He's a lively lecturer and although most of the orthopaedic techniques he demonstrated seemed designed to put GPs off performing surgery in their practices it was at least entertaining. More importantly, I was able to use the opportunity to talk to him about Isabel.

Walking down the corridor with him after the lecture I stressed how important I felt it is for her operation to be performed as soon as possible. I filled in the background of her personal situation which I hope will also help to make a stronger case for swift action. David was very positive and reassured me that he'd now succeeded in dovetailing the arrangements for the operation and aftercare in the disabled unit.

I don't feel that yet another of my afternoons off was a complete waste of time, having sorted that out. I'll be able to see Isabel tomorrow and give her the good news.

Opposite: Three months later:
Isabel with her new knee

SATURDAY
3
FEBRUARY

DRIVING ALONG THE tortuously twisting roads over towards Halton Ghyll today I got stuck behind a rusty old Mini van. After a couple of miles trying to pass it I became aware of a pair of eyes peering at me through the small rear window. Eventually when I overtook the slow vehicle the sunlight was reflected through the van, revealing the owner of the eyes to be a goat. It was a large animal which couldn't have been crammed into a much smaller means of transport.

The animal's predicament reminded me of a wonderful farmer friend back in the Sixties, who sadly died of a brain tumour several years ago.

Benny Morehouse farmed at Gisburn and I've experienced one or two nights out with him and his fellow farmers, when a few pints were downed. He was a great raconteur, with a wonderful ruddy laugh. I heard more than once how Benny had been out on the town till the early hours, but was back at work before most others the next morning. 'He'd 'ave sold more meat by the time Tom arrived, than Tom would sell in the rest of t' day,' was a stock remark of respect from his colleagues.

Not long after I'd arrived in the area to practise, and had just started to get to know Benny, I had a call from Skipton police telling me my presence had been requested by him as his defending doctor. I knew vaguely what the innocent-sounding title involved, but hadn't undertaken the duties before. It was a pretty thankless task and one which you soon learned to avoid.

Benny had been stopped by one of the bobbies for being drunk in charge of a vehicle. This was long before the introduction of the breathalyser, and the degree of inebriation was assessed by a police surgeon, using tests which were hardly sophisticated in forensic terms. The accused had the right to call in his own doctor as an observer, who I suppose in theory was there to see fair play and argue the case for his patient.

I was shown down to the cells where the police surgeon was gathering his extensive and sensitive instruments. They amounted to a pen, a penny and a straight line.

Benny's whereabouts were easily pinpointed by following the sound of quiet, tuneless humming, punctuated by gentle hiccups. He sat behind the bars of the only occupied cell with an innocent smile, looking out on the proceedings with a benign air. Knowing

Benny it wasn't difficult to recognise a typical post-hostelry state, fairly deep, but controllable in his own way.

Without needing any resort to such unpleasant items as keys, the cell door swung open. Benny shook my hand, and I helped him off with his coat and said we ought to get on with it. There was no doubt he was well over the limit, but the tests had to be performed as prescribed by HM Government.

1. *'The accused will walk in a straight line'*
Benny stepped across to the start of the first test. Forgetting everyone else in the room he weaved his way along the line, with the concentration of an acrobat walking a high wire across the Niagara falls. His confident air was replaced by a look of intense determination which deepened with each step. If his bodily rather than motoring life had depended on retaining his balance, he couldn't have put much more effort into counteracting the wobbles. So great was the illusion created that at one point all three observers flinched at a particularly violent lurch, and were only just able to stop themselves reaching out to save him.

2. *'The accused will pick up a penny piece placed on the floor'*
I think the main problem for Benny here was which penny to go for. The origin of his confusion was clear. The police doctor had explained that he had to pick up the penny lying six feet away, but Benny realised this was a trick. He could see two coins. Possibly deciding on stealth as the best approach, he moved slowly out of his chair, taking care not to surprise his quarry lest they make a bid to escape. Then he lunged for the money. I have no doubt he would have succeeded had he not attempted to pick up both pennies at the same time.

3. *'The accused will write his name and address'*
I felt he excelled at this one. There was a fair amount of heavy breathing as he sat resolutely hunched over the table, but he managed a passable impression of a doctor's prescription scrawl on a bad day. Had this graphological sample been the only means of testing the degree of his intemperance he might well have been given the benefit of the doubt by the two medics present. After all, most doctors' handwriting is hardly an example of impeccability.

I couldn't help glancing across at John, the police surgeon, who I knew well, and raising my eyes. Despite the last minute rally it was hardly a cliffhanger of a case.

As Benny slumped back into the chair, exhausted from his minutes of intense concentration, the police surgeon said, 'Right, Benny, thank you, that's the test completed.'

'Well, am I sober or what?' asked Benny in a triumphant tone.

'I'm sorry, but it is my opinion that you have imbibed a considerable quantity of alcohol, and you are over the limit at which you should have stopped driving.'

Benny looked astonished. He had clearly been convinced of his sobriety. Hatching some plot or other in his mind he looked across at me hopefully, but before he could say anything I just shook my head.

He didn't say much, just, 'Oh,' accepting my 'Nothing I can do to help' shrug in a philosophical manner, and shrugging back an implicit, 'Well you can't win them all.'

Not being one to dwell on things, his spirits rose.

'Well, can I go now?'

'Yes, sir,' replied the policeman behind the desk.

'Can I have my car keys, then?'

I don't think the policeman could believe the good-humoured audacity of the man.

'Well, no, Sir. You've been found to be unfit to drive.'

'Oh,' replied Benny. He thought for a moment. 'Well, can you give me a lift home, then?' By now the police had warmed to him and were quite happy to provide a taxi service.

Outside Benny walked over to his car and stood by the passenger door expectantly.

'No, Sir, we'll take one of these,' the constable said, pointing to a police car.

'Oh well,' said Benny, shrugging his shoulders. 'Have you much room in the back?'

This puzzled the young bobby. 'Why, Sir?'

Benny went to the back of his big black Ford and opened the boot. 'Well, you'll have to take this bugger as well.'

A loud bleat heralded the appearance of two large ram's horns. Benny had been on his way back from the mart, having loaded his newly acquired tup into the boot of his car, when he

·53·

decided to stop for the fateful jars. The poor animal had ended up incarcerated for an even longer period than Benny.

I suppose we shouldn't have been shocked when it made a bid for freedom, but its athletic jump over the rim of the boot did take us by surprise. Policeman, doctor and criminal then spent an interesting few minutes chasing the tup around the car park. It wasn't going to let a few humans stand in between it and possible food, which it perceived to be in the direction of the main street.

It was Benny who cornered the tup and deftly grabbed him to a standstill. Unfortunately such skill was not permissible evidence in his case, otherwise a reprieve might well have been forthcoming. The officer in charge decided a police car was not the ideal conveyance for a frisky tup, and reversed his original decision not to take Benny home in his own car.

It took three police constable reinforcements to help wrestle the tup back into Benny's car boot, and a fourth with a huge grin to drive the car home, followed by a police car so that Benny's driver could be returned to his more normal duties. So Benny had his tup, his car, a police chauffeur and a Yorkshire constabulary car to escort him home to Crow Park Farm. His benevolent smile broke into one of his hearty laughs as the convoy turned in to the farm gate. Whatever would Betty be thinking when she saw this lot approaching from her vantage point in the kitchen window?

Some few years later this marvellous character had me puzzled yet again, but this time it proved to be the brain tumour from which he died. And sadly only the other day burglars broke into Betty's home and stole all the jewellery that this great, laughing and lovely man had given her those memorable years ago.

MONDAY

5

FEBRUARY

I SANK MY GIN AND TONIC with even more than my usual fervour this evening when I finally returned home.

I'd spent over an hour, late in the evening, dictating notes, sorting out queries and hospital referrals from a long list of today's patients. When I replayed the blasted tape machine to check the last entry, it took off on a mad journey on its own initiative, spooling backwards for no apparent reason. I eventually stopped it with a sharp bang on the desk, something which the film crew tell me is called 'percussive maintenance'. The machine must have taken extreme umbrage at this heavy-handed treatment because when I managed to get it to move forwards again, the wretched thing wiped everything I'd done, barring the first two words.

An hour's work wasted, and at the end of an already long day, drawn out by yet more work connected with the Government's wretched new contract for GPs. We had an hour and a half's meeting this afternoon to discuss our implementation of the new proposals about child surveillance, which took up the time I'd set aside for catching up with my pile of correspondence.

However, this evening, after a few well-chosen expletives, I went back to the top of the pile of patients' notes and hospital referrals and dictated the whole lot again. I added a message to Ann, our secretary, to excuse the thunderously black tone of my voice, telling her the reason for the occasional temperamental outburst.

I was already pretty tired after another busy twenty-four hours on call, my fourth night on in the last five days. We're short of people this week, with Eric on a skiing holiday, Clare away having had her baby, and Bill down in London again on his MSc course.

I had finished my surgery list at about seven o'clock this evening, after an eventful afternoon thanks to Michael, a sad but likeable character who is prone to outbursts of bizarre behaviour. This afternoon he'd turned up at the surgery in a very confused and depressed state. I told him to hang on while I finished with another patient but by the time I called for him he'd disappeared from the waiting room. We searched the building for him, but he'd obviously scarpered. I phoned the police, who also know Michael, and they sent out a few of their lads to look for him in

his usual haunts, but they had no joy either.

I had to finish off my surgery, but Michael was at the back of my mind all the time. I was pretty sure that, even in the state of mind I'd seen him in, he'd come to no harm, but I didn't like the thought of him being on his own. I was getting to the point where I thought I'd have to call in one of the others to finish off my surgery so that I could go and help look for him when the phone rang, and Elizabeth, who was on reception, told me he'd been found waiting quietly in the town hall. He told them he'd locked himself out of his flat, something he's prone to doing, and needed help to get back in. Last time it happened we had three keys made which we placed at strategic points, but they all seem to have disappeared.

I finished surgery and nipped out to see how Michael was doing. He lives on a council estate and as I pulled up outside his block of four flats I could see the upstairs lights were on. I climbed the stairs to his front door, following a trail of wood shavings and sawdust. The council's emergency locksmith had obviously been very prompt and, judging by the appearance of the door, had hacked out the old lock and fitted a new one. I knocked and the door opened under the gentle pressure. The strains of music which drifted around the flat from a radio in one of the rooms made me feel happy that someone was at home. I shouted his name. No reply.

I knocked on the living room door and went in, expecting to see Michael asleep. Instead, all I saw was the gas fire burning away at full heat, and the radio in the corner playing quietly. There was an element of the *Marie Celeste* about the place. A brief search of the rest of the flat revealed no sign of Michael, despite the fact that all the lights were on.

This made me feel uneasy. I didn't like the idea of him wandering about in the state I'd seen him in earlier. Across the hallway I knocked on Lilly's door. No reply or sign of life here either, which was actually a good omen. The two of them some-times wander up into town together. I hoped that they were having a cup of tea somewhere.

To be on the safe side I called in at the police station on my way home to find out if they'd seen Michael at all. The sergeant explained that they'd been down with him to make sure the lock was changed, and when the job was finished and he was back inside with the fire going they'd felt happy leaving him there, seemingly in a far more relaxed state. The sergeant said he would radio their cars to keep an eye out for him again.

There wasn't much more I could do and as I was on call I thought the most prudent thing would be to get some food inside me.

I ate my meal in peace, but at about 10.30 p.m., just as I was settling down to a loud helping of Elgar on the CD player, the phone rang.

On the other end of the line a tired and worried-sounding Vincent explained that his wife was in trouble. We've been treating Doris for years for an amazing variety of ailments. Most recently she'd developed what are most easily described as varicose veins in her food pipe. She'd been vomiting and the veins had started to bleed very badly.

Driving to her house in Ingleton, a village about 10 miles

away, I had time to think about her medical history. She had acute renal failure seven years ago and had bravely suffered her share of hospital investigations since then. From the sound of the call, things might have fallen apart again, and I'd already put an ambulance on standby before leaving home.

When I arrived, the front room curtains were open and the light shining to guide me up the road. Vincent's stocky figure was standing in the doorway looking out and as soon as he saw the car he came to the door to greet me. I was ushered in and asked to go straight up to the bedroom.

There was only a dim bedside light casting deep shadows across the room, but I could just make out the top of Doris's head poking above the covers. Having switched on the central light I knelt beside her and gently felt a rapid and rather weak, thready pulse. Doris was shocked and understandably anxious, but still managed a small smile as she realised it was me. She fumbled for her glasses as I asked her what was up.

In a barely audible voice she told how she had started vomiting an hour before, and more and more blood had been appearing each time. When she spoke her exhaustion was obvious.

As I examined her, she continued to tell me how she had been over the last few hours, and as I carefully listened and nodded she almost visibly relaxed. She and Vincent were both aware of the most likely course of events. She wasn't in any immediate danger, but if the blood loss continued, as looked likely, things could become dicey later.

'You know what I'm going to say, don't you?' I asked the two of them. A nod from Vincent and another weak smile from Doris. I explained how it would be better if she went into Airedale Hospital so they could keep an eye on her. Better to move her now, than have a shocked patient who had lost a lot of blood on our hands in a few hours' time.

IT WAS 11.30 P.M. by the time I left the house, having called the ambulance, phoned the hospital, written a note for Doris to take with her and made sure she and Vincent were both more relaxed and understood what was going to happen. As I drove home along the back roads I saw the ambulance going in the direction of the house. I wanted to call in at Michael's to make sure he was home safely.

As I drove up I could see the lights were on, apparently just as they had been before, with the curtains wide open. From the outside nothing looked different. At the top of the stairs the efforts of the locksmith were still in evidence, and the door was still open. I pushed it and called out as I entered. This time there was a muttered reply. I entered the front room, not quite sure what to expect. Michael sat on the sofa smoking a cigarette and looking like a limp rag doll. His hair hung raggedly over his face. The papers and old coffee cups which had lain strewn across the room were still in their same places, and the gas fire was back on at full blast. 'Hello, Michael lad. Where have you been?' He looked up as I spoke. His eyes turned towards me in such a trusting way it would have been enough to touch even the hardest of hearts.

I discovered he'd been up to The Falcon Hotel for a cup of tea. He works there helping to clean several days a week, and I suppose it was a natural place to go.

Just before midnight I left him, feeling a great deal happier that he was going to be all right. It seemed most likely that the afternoon's adventures could be put down to a reaction to losing his keys and getting upset about the situation.

THE REST OF THE night was uneventful, thankfully. The good people of Settle and district were obviously sleeping soundly, peacefully and healthily for one night.

WEDNESDAY

7

FEBRUARY

IN MY MIND there are two types of heroism. First, there is the sort where someone selflessly jumps into a river or runs into a burning building to save another's life. That's raw courage, easy to see and understand. Without meaning to decry bravery of that kind, the other kind of courage displayed by some of my patients is far less obvious, but immeasurably more moving.

Josephine Eccleston exemplifies such courage. She really is a remarkable woman.

Over a year and a half ago we found she had ovarian cancer, which has been treated with chemotherapy. She'd been doing really well until suddenly a couple of weeks ago she wavered a little. There were no precise clinical signs of this. Caring for and observing these patients is a little like sailing a dinghy in a light wind. You just sense rather than see a change in the patient as a result of pulling together many small observations.

I spoke to Dr Michael Crawford, Josephine's chemotherapist at Airedale Hospital, and told him that I felt something was different. This was confirmed last Thursday when Francis, Josephine's husband, took her down for her weekly session. Dr Crawford told them the latest X-rays had shown that Josephine has developed metastases, secondary deposits in her lungs, which are now making breathing difficult for her.

At this point a good many people would have given up and wallowed in self-pity. Not Josephine. She's always pushed the rest of the family along and not let them get maudlin about the situation. It's not that she's burying her head in the sand, very much the opposite. She's facing up to the realities of what lies ahead, and is determined to live every moment of the life left to her to the full. Francis was telling me this evening that they'd both been up in town two nights ago dancing, and last night they were playing dominoes at our local pub. Josephine took great delight in detailing how she'd won. This positive attitude has been vital for her family who are understandably very upset by the latest bad news.

This morning, however, things didn't look so bright. One of her daughters rang to say Josephine had been found distressed, short of breath, and – most disturbing to the family – almost delirious and talking irrationally.

As I examined Josephine I wondered if this might be a terminal event for her since she was having terrible trouble breathing, with very wet and congested lungs. There was an element of what we call toxic confusion – a combination of fever and infection – with heart failure, secondary tumours in the lungs and possibly also in the brain. All this would understandably lead to the bizarre talk which had frightened everyone so much.

I treated her energetically by both intravenous and intramuscular routes which seemed to have the desired effect, for after sleeping for several hours she felt better and we'd managed to dry out her chest quite a bit. By this evening she was sitting in her dressing gown downstairs on the couch with her family around her. There were three daughters, a son, two grandchildren, Josephine, her husband Francis, and their old sheepdog, Laddie.

In some people the loss of hair caused by chemotherapy is hard to ignore, and it is difficult to prevent your eyes from focusing upon it. With Josephine, her smiling face and strong voice make you unaware of anything out of the ordinary, and her personality does more than any wig could ever do to make up for the physical changes. In fact it struck me that from her demeanour she might easily be viewed by a stranger as someone recovering from no more than a minor twenty-four-hour bug.

She was back on good form, laughing about some of the crazy things she'd been saying earlier. I did little more than sit with them, a glass of Fran's own special medicine in my hand, and talk. Dr Crawford the chemotherapist has told them they now have a decision to make: whether to try further chemotherapy for Josephine, or to remain on the drugs she is presently taking, which will only help her symptoms.

They asked me for my opinion. It's always difficult to give advice about these types of decisions – all you should really do as their doctor is to help them make up their own minds by talking through the implications of each course of action. In this case an increased chemotherapeutic regime might give Josephine a few months longer, but would almost certainly have severe side effects which would make her pretty ill during the treatment. I'm fairly sure I know what their decision will be, having heard Josephine speak about quality of life several times during the last few days.

In her wonderful rich accent, a mixture of her native Northern Irish and the Yorkshire she's picked up, she talked about it again, glancing at Francis for signs of confirmation as she spoke.

'I've said before if it were going to make me very, very ill, and it weren't going to prolong things that much longer, I'd rather not have it. I'd rather be grand with the family, you know.' Francis fingered his glass as he listened to his wife. 'I know I had a bit of a crisis this morning, but I think meself I'd like my family to remember me like this rather than suffering from chemotherapy.'

We sat in silence for a while, her words floating in our minds. Then Josephine started to talk again.

'The family have been super, you know.' This wasn't said with any trace of sadness, although a note of disappointment crept in as she continued, 'I felt I'd let them down again when Dr Crawford told me about this,' she indicated her chest, 'last Thursday.'

I asked why she felt she'd let them down.

'Well because I've always been so determined; always said "Oh God, I'm not going to let this beat me. I'm going to overcome it." Then when he told me, I thought, "Oh God, I've gone and done it again, let them down," you know.'

Francis cleared his throat slightly and spoke in a distant, matter-of-fact voice.

'She's been on chemotherapy for virtually fifteen months now. Long time, isn't it.' And he looked down at his glass again.

Josephine carried on. 'Then I said, "Oh be bugger it," I says, "I'm still not going to let it beat me."'

We sat in silence again. Not a heavy, sad, or embarrassed silence, more of a peaceful quiet. Hard to explain really.

After a while one of the daughters told us about Steven, Josephine's five-year-old grandson, and his reaction to his Grandma's bad bout that morning. He'd been in to visit her each day, but this morning had come to see her and found her still in bed.

'I heard him go up and shout, "Come on, Grandma, get yer bloody self up!" and he climbed into bed with her.' We all laughed at her description of the colourful language from the five-year-old. 'Then he heard her terrible breathing and asked "What's she doing that for?"'

Above the laughter I murmured to Francis, 'There's some right bloody language in the Eccleston family!'

The little fellow then apparently stayed sitting on the stairs until it was time to go to school. His mother said that he was frightened at seeing Grandma ill, and knew something was up.

After I left the Ecclestons, Scottie and I went over to our friends Hugh and Joan Stalker's for supper, having given Francis the telephone number just in case. On my way home I called in again, and she was even better, which is encouraging.

On Friday I've arranged for Dr Crawford to visit them at home to speak to the family about the future management of Josephine's illness. Before and after then she's going to need all the support she will undoubtedly get from the rest of the family while she makes some difficult decisions.

THURSDAY

8

FEBRUARY

Dr Michael Crawford arrived at the surgery this afternoon so that together we could visit Josephine Eccleston. I have no doubt that a home visit by a consultant can be a marvellously useful tool in the management of patients and their illness.

I know that most consultants would like to do more such visits but cannot – largely because of the pressure of time. There may be a very few who prefer to stay in the sanctity of their hospitals where they can hide behind their white coats, and where their place in the hierarchy is assured and understood. Out in the sticks respect isn't so easily given; it usually has to be won in one way or another.

The advantages of seeing a patient in the home setting are immense. Observing the whole scene and understanding the mechanics of the family can often radically alter an opinion as to possible treatment. In Josephine's case I felt it was essential, to help explain the decision I knew she'd already taken about further chemotherapy, and I was sure that seeing her surrounded by her family would explain the motivation for this decision. I know it's not the case with Michael, but sometimes specialists may put pressure on a patient because they feel it's almost a personal insult when the treatment they offer is refused.

On the short journey from the surgery to the Ecclestons' house, I explained the problems we'd been having over the last couple of days and the drugs I'd been giving.

Josephine was sitting on the settee again, looking brighter than ever. An interesting discussion followed between Josephine, Francis and us two medics. Michael was asking how things had been since he last saw her. When had she noticed her breathing becoming a problem, and when did things really start going wrong?

Initially Francis did most of the talking. 'I noticed a change after visiting you last Thursday. This could have been us sat looking for things you'd told her would happen.'

Michael asked what she'd been up to, and Josephine had great pleasure in retelling the disco story. 'I didn't think my legs would go for me,' she said. 'I mean I could feel meself getting out of breath a bit but I got up again, and got discoing again. Oh, it were a great night.' From the smile she gave us both it obviously had been.

We agreed it was exactly what we wanted life to be for her. During the next few minutes the three of them ran through how Josephine had been sleeping, and Michael was able to piece together a picture of her health during the last few days.

Then I thought it was time to move the discussion on. I explained to Michael that Josephine, Francis and I had been discussing further treatment, and that we wanted to get it sorted out while he was there.

You might have expected a resigned attitude from Josephine and Francis as we talked, but there was nothing negative in the way they spoke. Francis asked for confirmation that more treatment would only prolong things for a month or two. Josephine nodded in agreement, saying that if he could just tell them about this again they could decide from what he said.

Michael glanced momentarily at the thick file of her notes on his lap, and started to talk about her case. I imagine that in a hospital environment referral to the notes would have been an obvious prop. Here in their front room, surrounded by photographs of the family, masses of flowers and the sort of ephemera we all collect over the years, it would have seemed out of place.

He ran through the discovery of her ovarian cancer, the eight courses of chemotherapy which worked in holding things at bay, with some small reduction in the tumour. Then the discovery of the cystic lumps in her abdomen which had become resistant to the treatment, and finally the metastases in her lungs.

Josephine and Francis listened to all this, nodding to confirm Michael's recall as he ran through her history.

He then went on to explain the options again.

'The chances of finding another treatment now to which the tumour cells are sensitive are extremely small.' Michael spoke in the quiet, assured tones of a professional used to dealing with clinical questions. 'As a figure pulled out of the air, let's say less than ten per cent. However the certainty is that you would have the side effects of the treatment.' Michael paused before continuing. 'The question is therefore would the kind of good you might get from the treatment outweigh the side effects?' Josephine was still listening to him with a look on her face which I can only describe as reassurance, almost as if she was telling Michael not to worry about straight talking. He concluded, 'At this stage I would advise not.'

Josephine looked at Francis, but without any hesitation replied, 'Well, that's all I wanted to know. Because I'd rather be laughing and joking with the family, you know, than be poorly.'

Michael reassured her quickly that it didn't mean treatment was ruled out completely, and that they would take everything as it came. We discussed the possibility of a blood transfusion which might help her anaemia and pep her up a bit, and it was decided to keep it in mind as a future action if she got to feeling a bit low.

Although there had been no histrionics, and everything was very positive, there had obviously been an intensity about the last few minutes. Now with this major decision out of the way the tension was broken by Francis asking if we'd like a drink.

'Tea or something a bit stronger?' he asked, looking at me, no doubt thinking of our several late evening discussions over a dram. At four o'clock in the afternoon with surgery starting three minutes ago I felt we had to refuse both.

Michael then cleaned the end of the Hickman tube. He'd inserted this into Josephine's main chest vein several months ago so that chemotherapy agents or other drugs could be administered directly to her circulatory system without having to find a vein with a needle every time. With the amount of treatment Josephine has been having it makes the process a great deal easier. I was able to use the tube yesterday when I gave her the drugs to help her breathing.

Josephine laughed and made some comment about 'warming it, please' as Michael took out his stethoscope to listen to her chest.

When we were sure we'd covered all the areas of discussion they were interested in we packed up. Michael rounded off by saying we'd leave it until next week to see how things were going before making up our minds about a transfusion.

As we were leaving, Josephine's three daughters came in. They were obviously in a state, asking about a new drug they'd heard about for cancer. It's one of the sad aspects of all the media coverage of any new medical development. In some of the less responsible newspapers 'miracle cures' are announced, when in fact these might still be nothing more than theories in a scientist's head. Josephine's daughters had heard or read about some such instance and quite understandably they were concerned that we hadn't tried the new drug on their mum.

We sat down again and explained that she'd had every treatment known to have results on her condition, and that the new drugs they'd mentioned were hardly at the trial stage yet.

After a brief silence one of the daughters said tearfully, 'I can't believe it's all over.'

We were quick to say it wasn't.

They'd been madly decorating her bedroom when she had had the bad patch yesterday. There were chuckles from Josephine about the decorating and, amidst the tears, promises it would be finished by tonight. Apart from laughing, Josephine hadn't joined in any of this conversation. Then she said, 'I don't know where I get me strength from but I'm not frightened.' Looking up at her daughters, and smiling, she continued. 'That's the only way I can help, really.'

They're a very close family, and the daughters have quite rightly been pushing both Michael and me to do more. The problem has been to reassure them that we have been, and are, doing everything possible. Through her tears one of the daughters told Michael about a recurring dream she has. In it he rides up the road in a white Rolls Royce and comes to the door with a small pill which he holds up to them as the miracle cure for their mother.

There was little to do except reassure the family we would both be on hand to provide the best possible treatment day by day. However, we each knew that from this point on we would only be treating the symptoms, and this would largely be in the hands of the practice at this end. Whatever else, I promised Francis I would keep her comfortable but as wakeful as possible so that she could enjoy her family about her.

On our way back to the surgery Michael commented on what an amazing family they are. He said how impressed he was with the way they always asked the right questions, constantly looking for information, and how he admired Josephine's ability to laugh.

'If you're going to have a cancer,' he said, 'I suppose it's better to have a sense of humour with it.'

AFTER A QUIET NIGHT on call last night, I awoke to find myself a year older. It's not just any old birthday, but my sixtieth. Amongst the presents and cards was a parcel from my old friend Denis Lockhart. Denis and I read our medicine at Trinity College, Dublin, and many's the pint we lowered in Dublin's bars in our carefree student days.

I couldn't work out what his parcel contained until I unwrapped it fully to reveal a flag in the colours of the Royal Army Medical Corps. Looking at this most appropriate present I realised I wasn't quite certain which way up the flag should fly.

A phone call to 201 General Hospital in Newcastle, my TA unit, revealed a gap in their own knowledge of our regalia. After listening to my problem the steward put the phone down on the table and I heard the click of his heels disappearing down the long stone floor of the hallway. I have a vivid image of him nipping outside to look up at the flag which always flies above the building to check the correct configuration.

I suppose it must be the time I've spent with the services, but I've always felt a stirring in my heart whenever the excuse arises to run some colours up the flagpole in our front garden. It's become quite a tradition on special occasions. It came into its own as a way of announcing the birth of each of our three children. We had two flagpoles then, and one flew the Union Jack, the other the cross of St George. I hope no one misreads the signal today and thinks that Scottie has produced again.

THE DAY CONTINUED WELL until the mother of a ten-year-old boy phoned me in quite a state, to talk about her son. She's understandably upset.

Two weeks ago Duncan had been found to have a tumour called an angio-fibroma which was growing and occupying the space at the back of the nose. Originally his mother had been promised he would receive further attention within a fortnight, but when she'd phoned the specialist's office she had been told Duncan wouldn't be seen for at least another three weeks. I spent the next hour on the phone trying to find the reasons for the delay and attempting to get an earlier appointment.

Whatever the reasons, ultimately they must come down to a lack of money. This may have come about because of actual cuts like the closure of wards, alternatively, or even in addition, it may result from the increased pressure on the Health Service brought about by the amazing new techniques and treatments now available in many areas of medicine.

The cost of treating illness has risen at a far greater rate than inflation because the techniques and equipment used are now so complex, and people's expectations are so much greater. When I was training in hospital thirty or so years ago we didn't undertake coronary bypass operations or hip and knee replacements, or many of the other treatments we now take virtually for granted. Today, quite correctly, we expect these illnesses to be dealt with as a matter of course. What we as a nation must face up to is the need to spend a greater proportion of our Gross National Product on health. After all, health is primary, without it little or nothing can be achieved by an individual or a nation.

In this morning's case, the lack of enough specialists and facilities to secure early treatment for their child was almost painful to report to the family. I only really succeeded in alerting the specialist to the psychological necessity of bringing forward the treatment, and I know he'll pull out all the stops to get Duncan an early appointment. Not really much comfort to the distraught mum.

THEN I HAD SOME bad news about Magdalene Ayres, the lady at Harden Bridge hospital with a hairline fracture of her left femur. So much for thinking she'd soon be back home. She had another fall, and this time she fractured her hip badly, and had to be sent in to Airedale Hospital. I feel so sorry for her, it must be very demoralising when she was doing so well. I must call in and see her when I'm down at the hospital tomorrow.

THE EARLY PLEASURE of my birthday having been dispelled, I set out for the branch surgery at Hellifield, stopping off on the 7-mile trip to see Colin Green.

Colin is a remarkable man who became paraplegic as a result of a dreadful pot-holing accident some twenty-one years ago. He fell when a link-piece at the top of the steel ladder he was climbing snapped, a quite unforeseeable happening which sent Colin's large-framed body hurtling to the uneven floor of the cave where he landed squarely on his back. He left on a stretcher with a fractured fourth lumbar vertebra and a transected spinal cord, which rendered the lower half of his body paralysed. From the moment of the accident Colin has maintained an attitude and philosophy which stand as an inspiration to all who know him.

He has an indwelling urinary catheter, and has to evacuate his bowel manually every third day. He has to be aware of the ever-present possibility of developing pressure sores on the paralysed lower half of his body if he stays in one position for too long. In order to try and maintain some tone in his paralysed muscles and joints he had a sturdy wooden frame built, into which he straps himself in a standing position for two to three hours a day, while he reads books and magazines on caving, mountaineering or travel. His bathroom looks like a gymnasium, so that Colin can heave himself around to lavatory and bath on ropes suspended from the ceiling. All this he does entirely on his own.

Until recently he has spurned the traditional disabled wheelchair for most of the time in favour of a four-wheeled machine which resembles a beach buggy. Using this and his specially adapted camper van he has been able to travel all over the country. He was telling me today that he's planning a trip to Scotland in July where he will travel the mountain tracks on his adapted four-wheel Honda.

A truly remarkable man who never ceases to remain cheerful. Whenever my world seems unfair, and I'm having a black day, I think of Colin and I don't have a problem any more.

HELLIFIELD BRANCH SURGERY is an administrative headache, something of an anachronism alongside our modern set-up in Settle. It's run from the ground floor of a terraced house in the village, the first floor being a flat which our trainee doctors use. Downstairs are the waiting room, a cramped dispensary and a consulting room just big enough to let one doctor and two patients in at the same time. With a full waiting room and a complete family in with the doctor it can become very interesting.

I like going there; it takes me right back to the days when the surgery was in my front room at home. We keep it going mainly for the old people in the village who would find the cost

Opposite: Colin

and the inconvenience of taking the bus into Settle too much to cope with. We don't run an appointment system there so you never know who is going to come through the door. This morning's queue was mercifully short, leaving me time to make another couple of calls on my way back to Settle.

Last call before lunch was in Airton. Marjorie is eighty-one and profoundly deaf, but she doesn't let that bother her. As I entered the low-beamed living room she was watching the snooker. As soon as she saw me she indicated the sherry decanter standing with the usual two glasses – a normal size one for me, and a smaller one for her, both of which she insisted on filling before I could start to examine her.

This ritual out of the way, I checked her blood pressure. Marjorie's just getting over flu and I wanted to see how she's recovering.

Her blood pressure was normal, the sherry was good and Marjorie as irrepressible as ever. We talked for a while about what had been going on in the village and in her life since I'd last seen her.

As I was about to go Marjorie rushed over to a wardrobe and pulled out her latest clothes purchases. 'What do you think of these?' she asked as she brandished them at me. I told her they were lovely and particularly suited her. Glowing from the approval, she gave me a huge birthday kiss on my cheek as I left.

One of the joys and privileges of being a GP in a rural practice is the degree of involvement which it's possible to achieve in your patients' lives. This is mainly because we don't just see them as medical conditions but part of a wider scene, in which we in turn also feature as members of that community. This demands a greater commitment to the job on our part and brings with it a set of responsibilities peculiar to a country doctor.

City doctors on the whole leave behind their involvement with their patients when they close the surgery door; likewise hospital doctors can cease commitment to the people in their care when they hang up their white coats. That is in no way to demean the dedication or professionalism of my colleagues in other areas. A small part of me envies their ability to leave their work behind when they walk out the door. Even when we are officially off duty we're still living by, if not over, the shop, so remain highly visible to our patients.

Although we actively discourage casual medical discussions in the pub or walking up the street, it's inevitable that we'll still be viewed as doctors first, and individuals second, even when we're socialising. Because of this prominence you can be sure anything said or done out of turn by any of us will be observed acutely and soon communicated to the whole area.

For these reasons I feel very strongly that a doctor in a small town has to accept a duty to maintain certain standards in personal life. Some may consider this an outdated philosophy, but it concerns me that some younger doctors don't always agree with this view. Although they may be fine clinicians and clever general practitioners, I still feel there will be one small part of their abilities missing if they are not able to demonstrate their own sound personal relationships. I'm not setting myself up as a paragon by any means, this is simply part of my philosophy.

One area in which I think it's vital to retain standards is in relationships with women. (I'm talking as a male doctor here.) I think we have to accept the fact that as the doctor or the vicar in a small community, our personal lives are on show, and that people still set store by what the GP does in his or her own life. We must remember however that our lives are no different, and we are just as vulnerable as anybody else.

The other important reason for taking care in our personal dealings with the opposite sex is that patients must feel totally safe in our hands, literally, without any room for doubt.

It's an attitude which should be picked up at a very early stage of medical training. Some young male doctors I come into contact with today seem to be frightened of dealing with the single female. In all my years I've only had a chaperone on two or three occasions. Those were when the hairs on the back of my neck were raised in warning, not that I was necessarily about to be seduced, but that someone was about to cause trouble for the sake of it.

The business of examining the opposite sex is really quite simple, and I suppose something most of us take for granted. Touch has to be psychologically cool and unsympathetic while clinically understanding. Thereby you receive in return the acceptance that your examination is purely medical, and the patient should be able to relax and put her confidence in you as a doctor. The general tone of the examination is important too; the eye contact and the turn of phrase, the sum of which help to complete the agreed contract of examination with no room for the slightest misinterpretation on either part.

The first time you examine a patient is inevitably with a group of other students and a consultant looking on. Any idea of this becoming anything sexual is never present. The predominant thought is the fear of getting something wrong from a clinical point of view, and in front of an audience.

I can't help thinking about an examination from my student days. There was a marvellous obstetrician called Tom Hanratty, with a soft, lilting Cork accent, who was running a Gynae teaching clinic one morning at the Holles Street hospital. An old dear was on the lithotomy couch where the woman lies on her back, her feet supported in stirrups with the legs apart to make internal vaginal examination easy. A small curtain was pulled across at the patient's waistline so she felt at least visually removed from what was going on, while the consultant could still lean around it and talk to her whenever he wanted to advise her.

This particular patient had been suffering from peculiar pain somewhere in her lower left half which she couldn't identify or explain. Mr Hanratty set one of our group to examine her and tell us what he could feel. In he went and spent a good couple of minutes feeling around. During this time, which felt like an age, Hanratty would occasionally lean around the curtain and smile at the old dear, muttering reassurances.

After yet more moments of silent concentration from the examining student Hanratty became impatient and asked in a concerned voice, 'Well? What can you feel?' Then he popped his head around the curtain and said with a big smile, 'It's all right, Lady, he's nearly finished examining you.'

The student replied he wasn't sure yet.

For obvious reasons it's not an examination anyone wants to become protracted and after a few more moments during which the student seemed reluctant to offer an opinion, and was looking decidedly flustered, Mr Hanratty asked, 'Are you going to let us have the benefit of your wisdom then, Sir?'

At which the poor fellow looked up and said in a loud voice, 'I think it might be cancer.'

Hanratty winced and muttered under his breath, 'Oh be Jasus,' and whipped his head around the curtain, turning on an even broader, disarming smile. 'It's all right, me dear, he's just talking clinical there. He doesn't mean you. Everyt'ing's grand.'

To rescue the situation Hanratty examined the lady deftly himself and within seconds revealed the cause of her pain. Triumphantly, like a slick conjurer producing a rabbit out of a hat, he held up a massive ring pessary. At that time these mechanical spring-loaded rings were inserted internally to hold up a prolapse of the uterus. This particular ring must have been in place for quite some years, since it was old, craggy and petrified like something out of Mother Shipton's Cave.

Holding the ring aloft so both students and patient could see, he turned to the student who'd made the cancer remark gaffe and asked. 'And what do we have here?'

'A ring pessary, sir,' came the reply in a relieved but embarrassed voice.

Hanratty turned to the woman and winked. 'I would rather call it the rear wheel of the menstrual cycle!'

At which the assembled group collapsed in laughter, including the woman. In making the joke he very cleverly banished all thoughts of cancer from her mind, while also making her feel one up on the junior doctor who'd made the mistake. I don't expect the student ever forgot the lesson either.

I HAD MY BIRTHDAY PARTY over the weekend. It was a great evening marred only by the disappearance of one of my presents. I'd left my newly acquired RAMC flag flying to welcome the guests. I thought to myself it would be prudent to take it in, especially when Eric Ward dropped in at about 10.30 on his way back from a call-out, and warned me that there were a few young chaps larking about in the square.

By the time I got around to going out to lower the flag I was too late, the flagpole was bare. I suspect it's been commandeered by some of the local lads in high spirits, on their way home from the pub. I felt very cheesed off about it, to say the least.

First thing this morning I drew a coloured picture of the flag on a postcard and put it along with a notice in the newsagent's window. It promises anyone who's 'borrowed' it an amnesty if it's returned. I'll just have to wait and see if there is any response.

AT TWO O'CLOCK this morning I had a call from Francis Eccleston to say that Josephine was in a bad way.

I donned my tracksuit and was at the house within minutes to find her gasping for breath, and really not good at all. I gave her intravenous therapy by way of the Hickman tube, and a small dose of diamorphine intramuscularly. Then I shifted her position a little to ease the pressure on her airway, and sat with her until she'd settled down.

AT 3.30 A.M. brave Josephine Eccleston lost her fight against ovarian cancer.

SHE EXEMPLIFIED dignity in death, to a degree I have seldom experienced. To the last she was cheerful and completely without fear.

To be honest, I had not been expecting such a rapid decline in her condition. After last week's problems, and her decision not to undergo any more treatment, I had hoped she would be able to relax and enjoy several more happy weeks. It proves how difficult it is to predict how the body will react, and reinforces my opinion that we should never answer the inevitable question, 'How long, Doctor?' with anything approaching a definite timescale.

In a strange way her death, although it was premature, doesn't leave me with any sadness. Of course I have immense sympathy for the family left behind, and understand they will be sad today and for a long time to come. Just yesterday she must have felt the end was getting near, because she gathered the whole family around her and talked to them for an hour and a half. I feel honoured to have known such an inspiring lady.

Since I remain equivocal about afterlife I think we should deal with the life we have and enjoy it to the full and to the best of our abilities within the confines of social and moral values such as honesty and trust. Quality of life is what's important, which is why I can't feel depressed about Josephine. During her last weeks she didn't just live within her limits, but, more importantly, right up to them.

In general I feel far more anguish from involvement with bad relationships than death. Situations where stupidity, a lack of understanding or communication have caused problems; where human insensibility has been responsible for much misery.

As I go around the practice I enter homes where love has clearly been lost or was never there, and others where it's very much a driving and exciting force. The difference is immense and obvious. I'm sure some of my experiences of both types of situation early in my career have made me appreciate my own relationships even more acutely.

I don't usually spend too much time examining my own feelings about death, but writing this diary and being so closely involved with someone like Josephine are both bound to prompt reflection.

During my time in the army I found I believed in something. I don't define it as God, but as integrity, sympathy, love, humility and kindness. I'm not a church-goer, but I hope I'm some sort of a Christian. I don't think there's any getting away from the fact that we're basically animals but we should behave as the most sophisticated of them.

I use the word philosophy a good deal when I'm talking, and I suppose uppermost in my mind is a respect for other human beings. This is a part of my religion.

Paradoxically, I believe strongly in the ceremonies of the church because I feel they have a symbolic role to play in society, whether it be a wedding or a funeral. Our culture has historically used these occasions as an opportunity to state intentions publicly and to mark important landmarks in the life cycle, especially the three main events: birth, marriage and death.

That's why I hate to see a poorly conducted wedding or funeral: it somehow cheats the central figures of their dignity. Funerals have an important function in the emotional aspect of death as well. They should be a time to celebrate the life of the person no longer with us and to mark their passing. They also play an important part in the grieving of friends and relatives.

When I have to cope with a particular death I like to jog off into the silence and peace of my favourite dale and make time to think and reflect. Scottie says I'm too much of a romantic.

INEVITABLY OVER THE YEARS I've had to deal with many deaths, but the death which still affects me most is one I had to deal with some fourteen years ago.

The whole incident is etched vividly on my mind. It was Saturday morning; I was off duty and just up the road in the pet shop doing some shopping when Scottie rushed in, having run the 50 yards from our house. As soon as I saw her I knew something was badly wrong. She grabbed me by the arm, and pulled me out of the shop as she spoke.

A woman in Horton in Ribblesdale had phoned saying her young son was suddenly having great difficulty breathing and getting worse every minute. We were back at the house by the time Scottie had told me the address. I jumped in the car and drove the 7 miles to their farm as speedily as my car had ever travelled. From the description of the sudden rasping breathing it sounded to me like a severe asthma attack and on the way there, as I usually do, I considered all my possible courses of action.

When I arrived I soon realised the best of my limited skills would be useless. The boy, who was but three and a half years old, was on the floor and very obviously dead. In a desperate attempt to do something we tried resuscitation but I knew from the outset it would fail. The ambulance team had arrived and we continued the attempts for a while but by then everyone knew it was hopeless. This handsome blond-haired boy lay dead and we had been able to do nothing.

It was a tremendous sadness. The parents, in their stunned state, told me that Brian had been a bit poorly during the night, but he'd got up late and his mother made him lie on the settee downstairs. He then complained of a sore throat and minutes later he'd started having problems breathing, until it got so bad they'd called me.

The post mortem revealed he had suffered a very rare acute infection of the epiglottis. This had caused rapid swelling, closing off the airway, which stopped the child breathing.

I've seen hangings and shot-gun suicides over the years and they each leave their mark, as do drownings and road accidents. But the violent suddenness of this event has affected me the most. This lovely little lad who had previously shown few symptoms was dead within half an hour. One of the joys of being a doctor is the feeling of being able to make people better. I suppose the very lack of any opportunity to do anything for that boy is why it still weighs heavy on my mind.

I was also affected deeply by what I felt was an inability to handle the grief situation. In retrospect I feel I didn't go back and help the boy's parents enough after the death of their son. As I describe this tragedy I feel I should return and discuss it with them. Writing about the incident may push me into doing so.

On the other hand I don't want to reawaken tragic memories for them, in a selfish attempt to make me feel better. All they might do would be reassure me that I did my job well, when I know I didn't. Nothing has affected me in a spiritual way like the death of that boy.

THE OTHER INCIDENT I've been involved in which affected me for different reasons in a deep way was a rail accident near Hellifield over eleven years ago. At about ten o'clock on a February evening in 1979 I had a call from the police asking me to attend the scene.

Two men had been out on snow duty, attending to frozen points on the main line. It was a filthy winter's night with a strong, icy cold wind blowing. The rule was for one man to keep lookout while the other worked. This night the points were frozen solid and the lookout turned to help. They must have dropped their guard at the precise moment that the Nottingham to Glasgow express, six hours overdue, came pounding out of the darkness, its sound and vibrations masked by the furious wind. It struck them both.

At the time I was deeply affected by the sheer physical violence of the whole thing. Death would have been instantaneous. The immediate task for me was to go directly to break the news to the families. It could have been left to the police but I knew both the men and their families; I had delivered some of the children into this violent world.

The men were aged forty-two and fifty-three. There was nothing for it but to go from one home to the next. In the first case I had to tell a wife and three children that her husband and their father was dead, in the second a wife and a mother. They of course had no idea anything had gone wrong, since the men had not been expected back before the following morning. The first indication they had that anything was amiss was me on their doorstep.

There are no set rules for dealing with these situations. You just have to judge each as it is presented, be flexible, and adapt to what's going on in the home when you arrive.

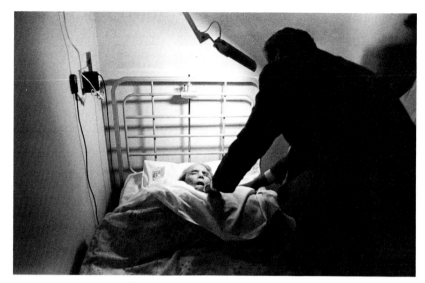

Death at Castleberg Hospital

It may be appropriate to make the smallest preamble but you must quickly offer a statement of fact about the death. The amount of explanation given at this time, and the answers you give to immediate questions, are all matters which you must judge carefully but quickly, appreciating the family mechanics and situation. The way you approach things will be affected by the presence of children, while if other relations are there you may use them to help the more bereaved members of the family.

Once you've broken the news, it is often best to let them work out their own grief in their own way by just staying silent. Some find it necessary to talk immediately, others remain quiet. Whatever the reaction, it's important to overcome the tendency to talk too much or stay too long.

The follow-up bereavement visits are vital and it is during these that we can begin to work through methods of dealing with the tragedy.

I've heard one or two people in the role of messenger recite platitudes. There can't be anything worse. The ability to remain silent is very important; it leaves room for the bereaved to ask questions as they take in the enormity of what has happened. Among the most often asked questions are 'Would he have died straight away,' or 'Would he have suffered'. Understandably people fear the death being protracted.

I feel it's very important to temper the answer to suit individuals, but it must be truthful. If possible I prefer to attend the accident myself or at least to have spoken to other professionals who were there. This enables me to give more careful information.

Whatever the details, no one wants to spend the rest of their life imagining the agonising last moments of their loved one. I take the view that whatever we say is not going to affect the dead person so why not help the people who are left behind to deal with their loss and their grief.

OUR LATEST TRAINEE, Dr David Pearson, arrived today fresh from Airedale Hospital, eager to start his six months in our practice. The scheme of vocational training in general practice began in the early Seventies and it involves bringing newly qualified doctors into practices for a total of a year to learn about the realities of general practice out in the field. Airedale Hospital was early on this scene and I became a trainer in 1971, partly because I remember my own naïveté when I had arrived in Settle with absolutely no experience of general practice, and was thrown straight in the deep end without really having been taught how to swim.

Even my home was thrust upon me; I had to buy the house we still live in because it contained the surgery. The front hall was the waiting room, separated by one door from the present dining room, then in use as the consulting room. I found myself in my small front room with a desk and an examination couch so low I had to kneel down on the floor to examine people's bellies. In one corner there was a green velvet curtain behind which I'd disappear to dispense the drugs from the 'pharmacy'. From that tiny room we'd mix up the pills and potions we used then; I'd try to write the patients' name on the waxed boxes (a nigh on impossible task), and give them to them as they left via the front door.

It was absolute chaos – just a hall full of patients; no appointment system. As one patient left the next would come in, and I'd have no idea who I'd be dealing with until a head appeared round the door. The records which were behind me in great files hardly ever left the cabinet because there just wasn't time.

Officially surgery started at 1.30 p.m. every day, but usually by 12.30 the first person would have come in and sat down so they had first place in the queue. Patients used to walk into the kitchen just before lunch when I was still out on my rounds and say to Scottie, 'Is 'e back?' On one occasion she was even disturbed by a knock on the bathroom door and a similar enquiry. This all put pressure on me to start surgery early when I did arrive home.

We knew no different, and trundled along like that for nearly three years. On Saturday we had surgery from 1.30 to 2.30 p.m. and again from 6.30 to 7.30. Two hundred yards up the road in his home, my senior partner was doing exactly the same! It wasn't too long before I began to evolve more sensible surgery hours, at least for Saturday.

The phone system was such in those days that our wives were on duty night and day. If I was on call Scottie had to stay in to sit by the phone. If she was on her own and wanted to nip up the road to get a loaf of bread she'd take the phone off the hook and run up the street, so at least patients thought there was someone talking on the other end.

Looking back it seems so archaic I can't help wondering why it took us so long to rationalise the system. I suppose the enthusiasm of youth made the whole thing a novel adventure for the first few years.

However, as we acquired dogs and children the invasion of people into our home began to get a little out of hand.

So we turned the waiting room into my consulting room and divided the other room into two by means of a plywood wall. This wall separated the receptionist's office from a small waiting room, and communication between the two was by a stable-door type hatch. This opened up the new possibility of running an appointment system, and people now could come in and wait on rather nice antique chairs in some comfort instead of queueing in our hallway.

It was at about this time that we managed to afford the installation of central heating, which would have amused my predecessor who had a philosophy that if his patients would wait in his cold, draughty hallway for a couple of hours they must really be ill and deserving of his attention!

As the numbers of our dogs and children increased and our living space became more crowded, it became unbearable. I knew there had to be another way. Then early in 1970 I was discussing the problem with John Hutton, the creamery manager, and he told me that a unique old building in the town, called the Folly, was being vacated by its tenant. Built in 1679, it nestles behind the market square, looking wonderfully incongruous in its setting alongside the small cottages of the town. Its façade would be more at home on a country mansion, with its stone mullioned windows and leaded glass.

After a certain amount of detective work I was able to discover who owned the Folly and negotiate a rent for the ground floor. With more sheets of plywood I divided it into a treatment area, two consulting rooms and a huge waiting room.

My senior partner, David Hyslop, who was then in his early sixties, went along with my plan and at that late point in his career agreed to move his pharmacy and rooms from his home and join in with an appointment system. This must have been a major change for him and one which many people at his stage of their working lives would not have contemplated.

The appointment system worked very well, and best of all was the lovely feeling of finishing surgery, closing the door and walking down through the market square to my home. There I could pour my gin and tonic knowing that, barring emergencies, we wouldn't be disturbed until the following day.

However, a problem soon became apparent. Plywood does not have great sound-proofing qualities, and consequently anyone speaking in a consulting room in a voice above a whisper could be heard clearly in the adjacent waiting room. To overcome this we attempted to mask any escaping sounds by playing music, on a tape machine, and I treated our patients to Haydn and Mozart which I thought sounded rather fine in this ancient building.

It wasn't long before Scottie overheard the first appreciation of our sound screen from a waiting patient: 'Sittin' in 'ere's like bein' in a bloody mausoleum.'

Six years after we moved into the Folly, David Hyslop retired. At the same time the doctor running our neighbouring practice in Long Preston, Harry Clegg, also felt it was time to go. Suddenly I was faced with the prospect of taking on all their patients and it didn't take a genius to realise I had to find some new partners quickly.

At that time every Friday morning I used to zip down to Airedale Hospital and run the casualty unit from half past eight to one o'clock. It was a great system, although hard work, because it gave me a chance to talk to the consultants and visit my patients in the hospital at the same time. It also meant I could keep in touch with the trainees, and through this I knew two particularly well.

Eric Ward had trained with Dr Pamela Hogg in Settle, and I knew him and Pat his wife from meetings in the hospital. John Lewis had been my own trainee so this was already a well developed relationship. We didn't have to look at each other for very long to realise it was a fair bet and they both decided to take up the offer and join me as partners. This was an exciting venture, with two young keen doctors set to enter the practice.

WHEN THE THREE of us started the new partnership, we each had a yellow Renault 4L, and one day I somehow got the idea of putting a black line longitudinally over the car on the driver's side. The object was to ease the problem of having to compete on the roads with the quarry lorries which heave their heavy limestone loads along our narrow highways. The drivers are very cooperative and when, in their mirrors, they see the black line on yellow, or white as it now is, they move over at the next available place and let us through. The spin-off from this simple plan has been remarkable, for we have learnt over the years that old and solitary people feel reassured in some small way as they see the distinctive doctor's car driving through their village. Since it is easily identified, patients will sometimes leave a note of some request under the windscreen wiper, a bag of scones or empty pill bottles on the bonnet, or an occasional brace of pheasants hanging from the wing mirror. The distinctive cars also help ambulance crews locate the house to which we have called them, and we are easily spotted as we arrive at road accidents.

Eric was first of the two new partners to arrive, six months before John, and he took over one of the rooms in the Folly. It was obvious that we wouldn't be able to carry on as we had been doing, and really had to consider ways to move forward.

I started reading up about other practices and suddenly hit upon a relatively new scheme by which we could cost-rent build a new medical centre.

First let me explain that there's an important distinction between health centres and medical centres. Health centres are planned and built by the Department of Health, and GPs rent rooms within them. For this reason such buildings usually function poorly, are unattractive and expensive. They are easily recognised by their flat roofs, and white roof surrounds, like Christmas cakes without the attraction of decorative paper frills around their sides.

Medical centres, on the other hand, are planned, built and paid for by the GPs who work in them and are usually functional, attractive and economic. The doctors can take advantage of a ten- or fifteen-year government loan under the cost rent scheme,

and end up with a building of their own. It's inevitably better built and designed than a health centre because the people who are going to use it have a vested interest in planning and building it to a high standard.

We set off around the country on visits to various medical centres to glean ideas. Crieff, Carlisle, Witney, Liverpool, Shipley, Wakefield and a dozen more came under scrutiny. Eventually we came across one which grabbed us and we got in touch with the architect who'd designed it. Chris Clair came to my home and we all sat around the table hour after hour on many occasions and discussed our plans.

Having visited a whole range of good and bad buildings we had a fair idea of what we wanted, and excitement mounted as the construction of Townhead surgeries got underway.

Townhead was the name of the grand old house which stood at the top of the 6-acre field behind my home. It was in its huge bay-windowed bedroom that I sat with old Tot Lord during his last illness, and looked across the open space to the town, not thinking I would soon be holding consultations in what was then a patch of nettles behind the graveyard. Townhead House is long gone but the weathercock from old Tot's house now rotates to the wind above my stable barn, and the surgeries bear the name Townhead out of respect for the old order of things.

We were very careful to consider the image of the place as people approach it, and include an interesting outline as well as a banked grassed area. The first room people see when they enter the building is obviously important, and we decided to make this waiting room large and light. Everyone seems to like it as much as we hoped they would, judging by the number of people who've asked to use it out of hours over the years for non-medical events, from wine-tasting to orchestral rehearsals.

We were definite about the style of the consulting rooms, designing them so patients sat beside their doctor rather than separated by a desk. After the experience of plywood partitions at the Folly, we also incorporated heavy internal soundproofing.

We decided separate examination rooms were important, so that if a patient needs a full examination we can take him or her next door to get undressed without haste and in dignified privacy while we can see another patient, which is obviously good use of our time. In this way, patients don't feel rushed either before the examination or after it, since they can also take their time to get dressed again without feeling they're holding us up.

The achievement of building the new surgery back in 1976 seems quite impossible now. John, Eric, myself and all our wives were deeply involved in its realisation, taking over every day after the builders had finished. We installed the insulation in the roof and under the floor, our wives did all the polyurethane varnishing of the wood – of which there is a considerable amount – and numerous other jobs to complete the fitting out.

By the time we'd done the year's work there was a strong bond between us all. The value was therefore far beyond the tangible end result of the actual buildings. It also helped to create a great sense of team spirit

The prospects today for young doctors like our trainee David are vastly different to those I experienced when I started out in general practice. Looking back, the process of learning and evolving all seemed damn good fun.

TUESDAY
27
FEBRUARY

I MET BRYN strolling up the street in Austwick, which was a good sign, and gave me an opportunity to observe his walk. I'm pleased to say it was very stable, despite the efforts of the windy weather. He didn't seem to be having any problems balancing, nor was he dragging his feet.

Bryn is now fourteen weeks post-operative. His wound has healed soundly and the only immediate problem is the effect of the steroids which he's taking to inhibit any swelling of the brain tissue after his operation. I could see he looked very swollen around his trunk and face. We have already been very carefully reducing his steroid intake, and I hope that will help reduce his puffiness.

Bryn, typically, joked that he'd be disqualified from the Olympics if he was drug tested. All in all he seems to have recovered well from a brief turn for the worse last week, and was back to his usual cheerful self.

On his last visit to the hospital they'd solved the mystery of the staples in the side of his head. When Mr Ahmed operated to remove the brain tumour, Bryn's head had been put in a cradle to keep it absolutely still. The cradle had caused a small wound which had been stapled together. This has healed and the staples have now been removed.

Bryn and Ann seem to be taking all the trauma of the illness and the treatment remarkably well. They certainly deserve all the support we can possibly give to help them cope with this continuing crisis.

THIS EVENING I've been to Airedale Hospital again, to score another Brownie point in the Government's training system. It was a lecture by some holistic doctor, the general theme of which appeared to be treatment of the whole patient and not just the symptoms. I'm all for keeping an open mind to new approaches in medicine, but I couldn't help feeling at the end of the hour's talk that most of the ideas being proffered as revolutionary were techniques we've been using for years. He was propounding the virtues of touch, talk and listen, which are some of the inherent parts of any good consultation. He talked of preventative care and good health as if no one else had ever encountered them.

I listened until I became a little exasperated and challenged him, pointing out that we'd been practising and evolving this very kind of medicine for years.

Nevertheless lectures like this evening's have the virtue of reminding me not to become complacent in my attitude to consultations.

After the meeting I called in to a psychiatric ward to see one of my patients who'd been in there for a few weeks. Betsy was sent to Airedale having become unmanageable at Greenfoot sheltered accommodation, where she was disrupting the other residents. She is anxious and depressed, as she has been for several years since the death of Albert, her mentally handicapped son. She treated him with such love and attention that she has never come to terms with his death; I don't think she's ever likely to, either. She's expressed her wish to die on many occasions, reasoning that she will only be happy when she can be with her beloved child again, and I believe she's perfectly right.

THIS EVENING, having examined and talked to Betsy, I met the doctor on the ward to discuss the difficulty of her treatment. She's got to the stage where she is not eating any more, and has not responded to any of the therapies tried during her weeks on the ward. The only option left with a real chance is electroconvulsive therapy, ECT, which she won't voluntarily accept. Basically it's an electric shock applied across the brain which can have remarkable success in helping to relieve depression.

I still believe fundamentally that Betsy will never be really content until she joins her son, but at least ECT will help her present state of mind whilst she waits.

I therefore signed a section 3 on the grounds that she's unable to make a rational decision about the treatment. Combined with the consultant's permission it will enable Betsy to receive ECT.

It must always be an uncomfortable decision for any doctor to take, to sign a section which compels his patient to receive a treatment which they have refused. However with careful selection of cases, such treatment is often most successful. I hope it will enable Betsy to enjoy some peace of mind.

FRIDAY 2 MARCH

WALKING UP THE ROAD to the surgery this morning a police car pulled up beside me. 'Morning, Doc. We've got something for you.'

The sergeant opened the glove compartment and produced a small plain postcard on which was written: 'On our return from Yorkshire the other weekend we seemed to have acquired the enclosed. We are returning it in the hope you will be able to reunite it with the owner. Our apologies!' No signature.

Once I'd read it the sergeant reached across the back seat and handed me one neatly folded maroon, gold and blue Royal Army Medical Corps flag. The lost, or 'borrowed', had been found. In a strange way I think the flag has taken on a new respectability in my mind. It's been involved in a minor skirmish and survived. No longer does it look like a virgin article drawn from stores; it now has a certain integrity of its own, imparted to it by the mystery journey. I hope that the people who commandeered it for such a brief period are reading this, and I take the opportunity to thank them for its safe return.

TUESDAY 6 MARCH

I WAS IN THE marketplace today buying my kippers, when I got talking to another fish buyer. I can't remember why the conversation turned to the subject of the Clays, but it set me thinking about them.

Harry Clay and his wife Jimmy were patients of mine for over twenty-five years; sadly, both are now gone. Jimmy's real name was Florence but for some reason she was known as Jimmy, a wonderful person with a fairly aristocratic background but as much at ease with a postman as a deputy lieutenant. She was a round, friendly woman who flirted with delight and who made everybody feel they were her favourite person. She died at the age of 87 and remained jolly and extrovert till just before her death. Jimmy had a most delightful way of putting things. I was in their kitchen once when Tony, one of their sons, who used to swear far more than I do, used a few well-chosen expletives. Jimmy turned to him and said, 'Darling, you really must watch your bloody language.'

Colonel Harry was a fairly quiet but jolly man, who had

commanded the local home guard during the war. I can picture him now leading his 'troops' around Giggleswick when I was at school. They were a real Dad's Army, complete with their staves and pikes in place of weapons.

The Clays lived up at Airton in a large bungalow with a dormer bedroom, and a big parrot. A real parrot, grey in colour, not like the smaller blue and green macaws or cockatoos we are more familiar with today. It used to sit proud and usually silent in an enormous cage. Occasionally it would attack the Colonel's finger when he was feeding it, whereupon some pretty strong language would ensue, first from Harry, then from the parrot which imitated him superbly. It was almost as though the bird provoked the outburst in an attempt to learn a new turn of phrase.

The parrot's infrequent talk was worth waiting for, and when it did flex its voice it was as clear as a human's. Every morning when Jimmy came downstairs she would lift the cover off the cage and the parrot would greet her with, ' 'ello, darlin', I *do* love you!' in its penetratingly high-pitched but precise voice.

One day the archdeacon and his wife came to tea. Jimmy got the full works out, complete with cucumber sandwiches. While

they were all sitting around the teapot, it started to snow violently as it can up here, and suddenly it became very dicey for the good church folk to leave, so Jimmy persuaded them to stay the night. What had started as an hour's tea visit turned into a long evening. During the course of this protracted stay, several stories were told, including a description of the eloquent morning greeting from the parrot.

As the evening drew on the Colonel longed for another large whisky, and eventually got it after the Archdeacon and his lady went to bed. Jimmy, being Jimmy, insisted their unexpected overnight guests retired to the Clays' own bed upstairs in the dormer room, while she and Harry slept on the sofa.

This apparently gave the archdeacon's wife an idea, for early next morning the Clays heard footsteps on the stairs, as Mrs Archdeacon crept down and tiptoed into the room where the parrot resided. They heard the cage squeak as she lifted the cover and imagined the look of delight on her face as the parrot took his cue and began his well-rehearsed greeting. ' 'Ello, darlin' . . .' There was an ominous pause as the parrot realised the face he was peering at was not his usual breakfast companion. In indignation he gathered himself together and screamed, 'Ah, piss off.'

The delight on Mrs Archdeacon's face must have changed to outrage, an expression which remained during a somewhat frigid breakfast and swift departure. As far as I know they never returned.

I REMEMBER BEING in the surgery one Friday just finishing the loose ends before I went away on a skiing trip. I heard the phone ring in reception, and was told it was Mrs Clay for me.

'Hello, Jimmy. What's the matter.'

'I think I've had a bit of a fall in the cellar, Dear Boy,' she said.

I couldn't imagine what this had to do with me but knowing Jimmy I played along with it. 'What's happened then?'

'Well it happened a couple of weeks ago, but it's suddenly got pretty bad today and it doesn't feel so good.'

When Jimmy said 'it doesn't feel so good' you knew it must be pretty bad. 'What signs are there?' I asked hoping she would reveal some information which would give me a clue to the problem.

'Well there's something sort of sticking out down below.'

It suddenly dawned on me she'd been describing a uterine prolapse. I burst out laughing at this wonderfully typical description from her.

I whipped over to see her and sure enough she had a marked prolapse, probably as a result of lifting something heavy. A few phone calls and my good friend John Phillips at Airedale hospital arranged to come out and see her with me that evening, and while I was away on holiday he took her in and operated. By the time I returned she was back to full power, telling everybody what a wonderful time she'd had in hospital, how wonderful the nurses were and how John, 'that darling boy', had been wonderful to her. He was to be sure to come up to go fishing with the Colonel on Malham Tarn, 'all arranged, dear boy'.

Having sorted her medical problems out she decided to go off for a couple of days on her own for some reason or other, a rare occurrence indeed, for she and her Colonel were almost always together. Harry virtually had to push her out the door because she was clucking around him so much, even though she would only be away for one night. He eventually shoved Jimmy in her car and said, 'For God's sake, woman, get off with you!'

Harry's apparently altruistic encouragement hid a black intention. There was a marvellous character called Arnold Lawson, who had become the Colonel's minder over the years – there was nothing Arnold wouldn't do for him. On this occasion, as soon as the sound of Jimmy's car had receded, the Colonel barked, 'Arnold! Get my gun and my stick.'

With great purpose and a determined look in his eye Harry led the way towards the dovecot. It had become overrun with pigeons which had been encouraged by Jimmy's frequent feeding. These relatives of the birds of peace had been getting on the Colonel's nerves. He could just about accept their cooing and their droppings, but could not accept a far more heinous crime. Not content with Jimmy's feasts, they had also been gorging themselves on the Colonel's newly sown field next to the house.

'Take my stick and rattle it around the dovecot a touch!' he ordered Arnold in his best military fashion. As the confused birds flew out, the Colonel picked them off one by one, until none remained.

When Jimmy returned she couldn't guess the reason for the

smug look on Harry's face, until she noticed the absence of the birds. Nothing was ever proved and less said.

I miss Harry and Jimmy; they were unique. Years ago Jimmy gave me a wonderful draughts set in a cabinet which had belonged to her uncle, a doctor in Harewood during the Twenties. One day he had been summoned to Harewood House to treat a weekend house guest who'd been involved in a minor accident. The temporary resident turned out to be the Prince of Wales and a few weeks later the grateful patient despatched the beautiful draughts set to the good doctor by way of thanks. Jimmy later gave Scottie another of her heirlooms, a brooch which once belonged to Florence Nightingale, knowing it would mean a lot to Scottie. We treasure both gifts greatly.

I wonder what happened to the parrot?

P.S. I've just discovered that the parrot is still alive, loud, and living in Calton; I can't be sure about the archdeacon's wife!

TUESDAY
20
MARCH

BRYN PHONED TODAY to ask me to visit him.

I've been really pleased with his progress, but yesterday he had a bit of a bad time. He'd been into Kendal to do some shopping and had been crossing the road when he fell. Although it didn't sound too much of a medical problem, he'd obviously been upset by it and I wanted to reassure him.

'What a bloody stupid thing to do, hey, Barry,' was his greeting on my arrival. Then he told me what had happened.

He'd started across the road when he noticed a car coming towards him. As is so often the way with people who are recovering from a major illness, Bryn forgets that he isn't quite as agile as he used to be. He decided to quicken his pace, but his legs couldn't keep up with his intentions and next thing he knew he'd fallen flat in the middle of the road.

He was still clearly unable to come to terms with what he saw as a weakness. 'How ridiculous. These two lads had to pick me up. They told me they could hear the breath being forced out of me when I hit the floor.'

He said he had no pain apart from a slight bruising around his ribs. However I sent him upstairs to lie on his bed so I could have a better look at him. I was pretty sure his inability to move quickly was related to the steroids he's on. Steroids can cause oedema, an accumulation of fluids in the body tissues. However it would have been all too easy to make this assumption, and overlook a new medical reason for Bryn's fall.

I felt his abdomen to make sure he wasn't suffering from any lumps or lesions in his belly wall which might indicate secondary deposits of cancer, or stomach ulcers which can sometimes be brought on by the steroids. There was no indication of any tenderness, although the drugs are obviously making him put on weight. 'I'm growing breasts like a Sumo wrestler,' he joked, as I palpated his chest wall.

I had to tell him to keep quiet as I examined him because he kept shaking with laughter as he joked about his physical appearance. But like a naughty schoolboy continuing to ignore teacher's orders, he kept on. His wife Ann joined in my pleas for silence, and after I'd persuaded him to keep quiet and still for a moment I was able to complete the examination.

The fall doesn't seem to have caused any physical damage,

nor are there any signs of additional medical problems. Psychologically, however, it has obviously been a blow. Bryn has been
recovering so well from the brain surgery that this incident has
served as a reminder of the seriousness of the condition he's in,
and it's bound to have knocked his confidence a fair bit. The good
sign is that he was angry with himself about the fall, and that
must help his fighting spirit. Bryn and Ann have been amazing
throughout the illness, maintaining a totally positive attitude. I
just hope we can continue to keep him on an even keel.

Having sorted Bryn out I visited Harden Bridge Hospital.
Through the window I could see three male patients sitting in a
line like the three wise men.

I was greeted by the nursing officer, Mr Beech. 'You're in
right trouble, you are,' he said, before I'd even shut the door
behind me. He explained that Willie Morphet had been complaining I'd kept him in for too long and he wanted to go home
today, at once. 'He wants to go back to fiddle about on his farm,'
said Mr Beech, with a smile and a shrug of the shoulders.

Willie had not been doing as well as I'd hoped with his broken
arm, although he'd eventually been persuaded to leave the farm
for a day to have another X-ray, and we'd subsequently been able
to help the infection.

After he'd recovered from these problems, however, he'd
generally deteriorated quite quickly and badly. His latest problem
was his driving. At the age of ninety-two he'd still been driving
his Landrover around to look after the sheep, when unfortunately
he'd had a spell of double vision. He had started to become unsure
which sheep to drive around, or which building to avoid – although
knowing Willie he'd rather have hit a building than a sheep.

He'd been out the other day when he'd seen a car coming
towards him, which had turned into two cars, and he'd not been
sure which one to avoid. In the end he'd decided to make way for
both and hit a stone wall instead. Obviously as soon as I heard
about this I had to ground him from driving anywhere, even on
the farm, much to his disgust. Then he'd become ill and went off
his legs for a while. It's just the general wear and tear of old age,
and all he really needed was some Tender Loving Care, which he

Opposite: Bryn

got as soon as I sent him to Harden Bridge.

On his second day there he was already up and about, pushing other patients into the corner of the day room in their wheelchairs; must be something to do with a herding instinct. According to Mr Beech he and my other two countryman patients had been putting the world to rights, especially in relation to farming.

Today Willie was only concerned with getting home 'back to Wig [Wigglesworth]', as quickly as possible. To the background accompaniment of an old black-and-white film on the television I listened to his chest, which was clear. Knowing that his good neighbours the Booths had moved his bed downstairs I was sure he'd be well cared for.

'We'll get you home tomorrow then, Willie,' I said, thinking he'd be pleased.

'No, I thought today,' he countered immediately, and in a tone which implied it was not a point open to discussion.

The only aspect of his return home which seemed to concern him was that the car which would collect him should come right up to the side door because he only had his slippers with him.

Having sorted out patient number one, we moved on to the second of the trio. Frank Beresford is ninety, and has been in Harden Bridge now for several weeks, having been sent in by my partner Eric Ward when he was duty doctor. Frank has had a couple of falls during the last few months and Eric had been called to his house by his daughter who'd found her poor father lying on the kitchen floor having fallen again in the night. Now we had a problem of what to do for him in the way of long-term care.

When I asked how he was today he replied, 'Champion,' in his rich farmer's voice, as he always does. I asked him to walk a few steps to show me how he was on his legs. Paul, our physiotherapist, has been helping him to improve his balance, and teaching him how to walk with a Zimmer frame.

When he was on his feet and about to set off I told him to take his time, and settle himself. 'Say a little prayer!' came the advice from George, who was seated beside him watching the event as intently as if it had been the finals of a sheep-dog trial.

Frank's balance has improved tremendously and I hope we can get him home soon. There's a bit of a disagreement in the family as to the best place for him to go. He obviously needs full-time attention which his daughter can't give him on her own.

Some old people find it difficult to tolerate being looked after, but Frank is one of those who respond well to care, and he would therefore be the ideal candidate for one of our local homes, such as Anley. However there is an understandable worry about finance. The sum of full attendance allowance and a pension doesn't necessarily add up to the full fee for private nursing homes or even residential homes. It's a matter which we'll have to resolve.

The last member of the trio was George. I'm concerned about him; he's now suffering from senile dementia and a general deterioration in his bodily functions. Before I could begin to talk to him he launched into a tale about how unhappy he is that no one is visiting him. Constantly sliding his right foot forwards and backwards across the polished hospital floor, he spoke in his deep Yorkshire accent, now tinged with an uncharacteristically bitter edge.

'She's just rung up to say she's not coming today, has Ivy.' Ivy is his wife, and he's obviously got it into his head that she doesn't care about him. And I know so well nothing could be further from the truth.

'I'm always last to be visited, and she can't get home fast enough.' He was looking past me into the distance. 'Her excuse today was that the rent man hadn't been. I said, "Can't you leave it with a neighbour." But she said no.'

Then he started to weep.

It's very sad to see him in this condition. I've known him a long time and, as so often happens in these cases, his personality has completely changed. He has lost all sense of reality and conjures up imaginary events, while apparently remaining oblivious to what is really going on. It must be very difficult for his wife who couldn't do more than she does. He forgets her visits and then becomes very aggressive about what he sees as neglect.

As Mr Beech and I stood in the corridor, I overheard the trio discussing my idea of getting Frank into Anley.

'When thou goest to Anley, thou goest to stay,' George was saying. 'The better end of the bloody poor live there, you know,' he explained with bar-room certainty to Frank.

Overleaf: Frank Beresford

'What do you call *this* place anyroad?' he continued. As we walked away I could hear Frank explaining that it was Harden Bridge. 'Oh, Tommy Harden's place,' said George, happy in the incorrect knowledge of his location.

It's difficult not to get disturbed when you see the effects old age can have on the body and brain. Sometimes when I have repeatedly seen an old patient, and in all that time there has never been a lucid moment, or a laugh or smile, I do wonder whether we've got it right. There may be no actual illness, the respiratory and cardiac systems may be in good order, and the patient may eat and excrete in a normal biological pattern – in short nothing threatens his or her life. On the contrary such patients are nursed and nurtured, and their unrewarding lives look set to continue as long as the moon shall rise.

Then suddenly a fever develops or a tumble occurs, and they are at last carried off by a hypostatic pneumonia, a severe congestion of the lungs associated with their immobility.

Happily and more often there is some glimmer of humour, a story to be told and listened to, and a glance of gratitude. Any one of these on its own or mixed with anything from frank aggression to weeping tears can make life somehow worthwhile, and give some reason for going on. But I have to confess to occasionally wondering if the Old Man isn't just getting a little forgetful himself, and leaving one or two for a little too long. Some of the aged seem destined to live empty and gormless existences to eternity.

A DAY WHICH HAS largely revolved around babies.

First task on my list this morning was to phone Helme Chase hospital, 29 miles to the north-west of Settle near Kendal, to ask them if they would be kind enough to accept an antenatal booking from one of my patients for her forthcoming birth. Most of our mothers have their babies in the obstetric unit at Airedale District Hospital, 25 miles away to the south-east of Settle, but the mother of this patient had only recently died in Airedale and understandably she's reluctant to have her baby in the same hospital.

On my way to some sailing on Windermere the other day I called into Helme Chase and was very impressed by the set-up. It reminded me immediately of the style of obstetrics we used to practise at Cawdor Ghyll Hospital, where we delivered our own patients until it was closed back in the mid-Seventies. Being a smallish unit the care was so much more personal, and the bonding relationship between mum, dad, baby and doctor was more easily formed.

Now in the normal course of events our mothers are looked after by the practice both for their antenatal and postnatal care, and are booked into Airedale for the actual delivery. Mothers are usually seen twice at the hospital before delivery, once in early pregnancy and secondly at about thirty-six weeks. After their baby is born they can elect to come home after two days or stay longer, whichever is appropriate to their physiological and family needs. In the meantime, during their pregnancy we look after them using a cooperation chart which the mother keeps with her, though we also have a card copy on file. In this way the hospital will have each mother's full antenatal history when she arrives on the labour ward.

Towards the end of this morning's surgery a new antenatal patient presented herself when Gail came in to say she thought she was pregnant. You have to pause at this point and sense whether the potential mum is happy or upset. In Gail's case there was no doubt: she was clearly happy about the prospect, but in the typical imperturbable way of farming people, taking it all in her stride.

Gail brought a specimen of urine with her, which will be tested for the presence of albumin and glucose, but not for pregnancy. The clinical signs of pregnancy are there and the reason for amenorrhoea, a missed period, in 99 per cent of cases is pregnancy, so there is no need to waste time and money on pregnancy tests.

Gail's pregnancy is exactly the sort of case which makes me feel content. I looked after her mum, Doreen, when she was pregnant with Gail, so it's a complete biological cycle. It goes back even further in this case to when Doreen came down to the area from Durham, along with five other girls soon after the war. They arrived in Settle to work in the kitchens at Giggleswick School. This sudden influx of interesting females caused a certain amount of innocent-eyed goggling from the boys, previously starved of any female contact in the monastic setting of a public school. Doreen in particular came in for much youthful praise, being a striking girl with black gypsy hair and lovely eyes. She married a local builder and proceeded to have nine children, of which Gail is the youngest. She has her mother's looks as well. I'll be pleased to help bring the next generation into the world.

This feeling of continuity has happened several times now. My very first home delivery when I arrived into the practice in 1962 was at Arnford, a remote farm some 5 miles from Settle. It's a grand farmhouse at the end of a long drive across the fields, way out on its own. Elizabeth, who is now one of our receptionists, gave birth there to her second daughter Susan, and it was a genuinely joyful occasion for family and doctor. In a way it christened my arrival in the district. I saw Susan on her twenty-first birthday when she called in to see her mother at the surgery on what seems like only the other day. In fact it must have been some seven years ago!

I regret the lack of involvement in the actual birth these days and miss the era when most of our babies were delivered at home. The bonding between doctor and patient is inevitably less now than it was when we looked after our mothers throughout their pregnancy. This afternoon I visited a mother and her baby who have just returned from hospital, and of course there was some bonding there, but the start point is way behind what it would have been had I attended the delivery.

There is so much advice given to mothers-to-be these days, and by so many different agencies, that I sometimes advise them to listen only to what our midwife and I have to say to them and ask us anything they like – then at least they have one point of reference. It is so important to get across to each mother-to-be that having babies is a perfectly normal biological process, and that the reason we see them throughout the pregnancy on a strictly timed regime is merely to establish that normality is continuing. It is also for this reason that the various blood tests, X-rays, scans and other examinations are done. It is in this context that the skill of obstetric care lies; the spotting of the first small signs that lead you to suspect any abnormality. If everything is going normally, and the mother is given proper prenatal care, then the delivery will almost always be straight-forward. The 'almost always' leads to the one truism concerning obstetrics: midwifery is normal in hindsight only.

In the days when hospital admissions were the exception, we would obviously have a pretty good idea of who was likely to produce when. The midwives would be called to the patient first, assess how 'far gone' she was and call us at the appropriate time.

Whenever I answered the phone and heard one particular midwife's voice my heart would sink, and I would take my time to get everything together. I'd know events would still be in their early stages because she made a habit of calling me too soon. But I'd still have to go out and see, just in case.

It was always a social occasion and I would end up drinking tea at all hours with several generations and branches of the family. I discovered early on that although it was good fun to sit talking with dad and gran all night over numerous brew-ups, I'd inevitably end up exhausted, and the surgeries and calls of the next day didn't cancel themselves. So if the delay looked like being considerable I would sometimes seek out a couch and have a snooze. As every medic knows, it is just when you're tired and off guard that the critical case will occur, begging the careful, wise and correct decision. So I learnt to kip down, having given instructions either to be woken when the baby's head appeared, or at a given time if nothing was moving. You didn't want to leave things too long in case problems developed, especially in the second stage of labour.

I've had one or two hairy times out in the wilds on remote farms in cases which by rights should have been normal, but turned in a surprise. Problems can arise from post-birth haemorrhaging after the placenta separates from the uterus.

Sudden and precipitous bleeding can be a pretty frightening thing to deal with when you're miles away from assistance. Fortunately it can often be resolved by the administration of a drug which reinforces the natural action of the uterus to contract and close down. Thankfully I haven't had to deal with too many such cases.

I think the one that concerned me most was the birth of Amanda. It was about two o'clock in the morning on Friday 13 March, 1964 and for one reason or another I hadn't got a midwife to help me. The place was a small house a bit out in the country and without a telephone. The delivery went well, having wound itself into a familiar routine. We'd started with tea, and the dad-to-be was whistling his worries away in the kitchen preparing a second brew in order to occupy himself. Amanda's head was on the perineum, ready to pop out, and her mum, Kathleen, obeyed my instructions to the word, relaxing at just the right time. The baby's head appeared, and then Kathleen pushed gently and Amanda was delivered without any tear to her mother's perineum. I clamped the cord and waited patiently for the placenta to be delivered, experience telling me not to be tempted to fiddle with the uterus in an unwise attempt to hurry things on. After a few minutes the placenta emerged and on inspection was entire, apparently with all the membranes present, so I knew that there were no remnants left inside the uterus. A textbook birth.

Time to tidy up and generally relax, look forward to the cup of tea and prepare to leave. It was still important to keep an eye on Kathleen because of the possibility of bleeding, as the uterus contracted. You learn to keep this stage of observation so apparently random that mother and father are unaware you are doing any more than packing up. Usually if all goes well the uterus closes down quickly with the help of some intramuscular Syntometrine and the doctor can go home to bed whistling happily to himself, having brought another life into the world.

On this occasion, however, a casual but routine glance at Kathleen revealed a tell-tale trickle of blood coursing from the vagina.

Immediately I palpated the uterus, which seemed to be contracted nicely; but still the trickle continued. I reassured

Opposite: Three days young

Kathleen, as I took her baby from her arms 'for a moment' and placed her in the cot. Then I injected a second ampoule of Syntometrine, but this time by the intravenous route, to speed up the final closing down of the uterus. I prepared to examine Kathleen in order to locate any local source of bleeding, possibly an internal, and unseen, tear which would need stitching. This would be a difficult enough operation in normal circumstances, but with only the husband to act as nurse, an even more unnerving prospect. The blood continued to trickle as did the sweat down my own armpits, and I don't sweat easily.

I went to the corner of the room and re-examined the placenta, thinking I might have missed a damaged area which could have remained inside the uterus, but it was, as I had thought, intact and entire. Then, just as I was beginning to run through the possible actions I would take, the uterus closed down and the bleeding stopped.

Resisting the temptation to shout some joyous expletive I replaced Amanda in her mother's arms with a smile, just as the proud father appeared with mugs of tea. I hope mother, baby and father were unaware of the dark patches under my arms, and the excess of adrenalin in my circulation.

Over the next few years home deliveries were discouraged by cautious committees and the Peel Report. The next stage for us was to start delivering our patients at the splendid small GP hospital called Cawdor Ghyll, 17 miles away from Settle, just the other side of Skipton. The nurses were caring and efficient, and would communicate well with the GPs. In the home environment I often had to rely on Gran's assessment over the phone of how it was going. From this description, often embroidered with old wives' tales, I'd learn to make a judgment on what course of action to take. Mind you the old wives weren't often far wrong.

The sisters at Cawdor Ghyll were very good, and most of them would judge the right moment to phone. I quite enjoyed haring off the 17 miles, which in the middle of the night took something around the same number of minutes. Often I would arrive just in time to apply a little bit of traction with a small pair of forceps to help with the last moments of delivery. Even on the occasions when the baby was already born by the time you got there, it didn't really matter. There was often some stitching to do, and it still meant an element of involvement in the birth which helped towards the long-term relationship. The nurses could also keep an eye out for bleeding or any of the other post-delivery problems.

This all meant that we could maintain our involvement but have the advantages of simple equipment, decent lighting and more constant after-care. However, occasionally some GPs tried to run it as a midwifery unit, undertaking inductions and using more complicated treatments. I saw my task as being involved only with the strictly normal side of obstetrics: 'Each man to his last,' is one of my favourite philosophies and we were not specialist gynaecologists. Even though one or two GPs were excellent obstetricians in their own right, once these sorts of procedures were carried out without full backup I really felt we were steaming into danger. I never hesitated to send a patient off to the specialist unit at Airedale, just 7 miles down the road, at the first sign of trouble.

Eventually, the closure of Cawdor Ghyll became inevitable. It was a sad day when we lost our involvement in the moment of birth. We still have to deal with death; we have a greater proportion of geriatrics to cope with; we even occasionally become involved in helping conception. But now that we have lost the immediate contact with the actual moment of a new life coming into the world, I can't help wondering how it affects the balance of our jobs. Who knows how much else was taken away from us in psychological terms. One of the privileges was always the involvement in the complete life cycle. As anyone who has seen a live, healthy birth will testify, it is one of the most uplifting experiences, even as a spectator, and no matter how many times you witness it.

Since our routine home obstetrics ceased, I've still been involved in few home deliveries, most of them unplanned. These unbooked cases are fairly stressing because the doctor may have no antenatal knowledge of the case from which to work. And sometimes the place of birth isn't the only thing unplanned either.

In one case a girl had been to visit Bradford and felt a stirring in her belly during the return car journey. She drove right past the entrance to Airedale Obstetric Unit, and home as fast as she could go. There she really started to feel ill. Her mother had sent her upstairs to lie down when she suddenly screamed the type of wail her mother recognised as the deeprooted pain of childbirth.

This must have been an extraordinary shock for her parents, who knew nothing about her pregnancy. Being a fairly well-built girl she had managed to keep it hidden from them. The girl's mother was a very sensible lady and, realising what was going on, she called me straight away. I grabbed what I could, pausing only to phone the midwife.

By the time I arrived, the girl's mother had appreciated the situation, accepted it, and had talked with her husband. He was waiting at the gate to signal me in, whilst upstairs she put some heating in the room and laid out towels. There was an air of magnanimity about these parents which helped their somewhat confused and frightened daughter enormously. I was at the house in quick time, which was as well, for the wee fellah's head was just bulging the perineum. Calmed and supported by her mother's attitude, the daughter cooperated very well, and delivery of her first baby, a super boy, was complete just twenty minutes after my arrival without her needing a stitch.

I put the baby in a drawer which I'd emptied unceremoniously of its contents, and lined with the softest items I could

find. Put by the heater the baby was quite happy, and there was no need for hospitalisation.

The mother and father who had become grandparents completely by surprise were sensibly delighted, and even happier when their daughter later married the father.

I sometimes wonder what it was that suddenly denuded general practice and family homes of the happy and worthwhile happening of having babies at home. Is it the expectation of perfection by society, coupled with the threat of litigation for imperfection, even though such imperfection might have been unforeseeable? At one time some perinatal mortality was expected, as I was strikingly reminded back in January by Millie, the old lady at Greenfoot whose leg I was stitching. Her story of the loss of her newly born child would not have been unusual, witness the section of the Hellifield graveyard reserved for the infants of that day.

Another force mitigating against having babies at home must be how the doctor's responsibilities are perceived. Today it's far less acceptable that a doctor may be 'out of the system' for several hours dealing with one patient in labour and therefore unavailable for his or her other 2000 patients.

The long-term effects on family and child of being delivered at home as opposed to hospital are very difficult to assess. I know that the feeling of closeness experienced by the whole family is far greater than when a new arrival is presented after a few days in today's sausage-machine style obstetric units. The faults lie not with the people who work in maternity wards, but with the system. Some mothers cope with the hospital experience very well; others come out feeling as though they've been almost irrelevant, just part of a factory process.

Whether over a lifetime this has any effect on the child we'll probably never know. Whatever the case, I will remember with happiness and some contentment the waitings, the anxieties and the joys I have shared in the homes of my patients with the midwives, my mums and dads and their families.

SUNDAY 1 APRIL I SAT DOWN in my study this afternoon surrounded by the ephemera picked up over a lifetime: several small cups won as a result of running faster than others in forgotten races at school or in the army; books taking me back to my student days; and, stuck in a log basket, rolls of maps and plans which chart the building of our new surgery along with the certificates which proclaim I am considered sufficiently qualified to practise as a doctor.

Those were presented to me nearly thirty years ago – years during which I've done my best to look after the people in my care, and tried to keep the practice up to date by incorporating new ideas, for the benefit of those same people.

Today, therefore, is a sad day. It is the day when the government's new GP contract has been imposed – a contract which we feel will no longer encourage us to work for a better service for the people of Settle. If anything it will make it more difficult to continue with the standards we have striven for up to now.

I have been moved to write to the local Conservative Association agent expressing my unhappiness at the way the whole issue has been handled and my fears as to the outcome.

This is what I've written:

Having voted for the Conservative Party all my voting life, I regret that I find myself compelled to resign from the Conservative Association.

My resignation is as a direct result of the insistence of the present government on forcing through the White Paper on health, and the General Practitioner Contract.

I do not think my own resignation will make very much difference, but I must insist that any party that barters with the nation's health is on a hiding to nothing, and this is just what this government has done. The implementation of the White Paper has been a dreadful exhibition of the worst kind of unreasonable and compulsive man management.

I have spent twenty-eight years building up what I consider to be a reasonable general practice. The White Paper and Contract will inhibit and compromise such

practices, and certainly will not improve the care we are
giving our patients.
I say again, no political party should barter with the
nation's health, because whatever else, health is primary.

I feel very sad that I've had to write that letter. I've been considering it for a while and have come to the conclusion that I have no alternative. We really must put more into health, and I don't just mean money. As a nation we have to realise that we need to become more committed to our Health Service because we have to accept that a country can't work without good health.

Of course the NHS does cost more than it did to run; medical and scientific evolution dictates that it must. Thirty years ago hip replacements were rare, now they're ten a penny and many other joints are replaceable. Transplants of many organs are commonplace, and whole new sciences have developed. More expensive drugs are being used as a norm and our society quite rightly expects this. Health does now cost more, but will always be fundamental to a nation's happiness and productivity, however much this costs. Ways of controlling this cost are another matter; but certainly the government's obsession with bureaucracy within the NHS management is proving counterproductive. The current situation can only be described as a bureaucrat's paradise, and it is costing millions in unnecessary salaries. We are being slowly turned into business-men, heaven forbid, governed by the cost of treatment and the profit motive rather than the best action for our patients. The future worries me considerably.

A more serious casualty of the new contract, certainly so far as general practice is concerned, is the goodwill that has been lost between the GP on the one hand and the necessary Health Service bureaucracy and Department of Health on the other. For some incredible and inexcusable reason the Department has just not reckoned with this vital factor.

There are some tasks which under our contracts we must do – having done those we could go home. I do not have to stay at the surgery till 7.30 p.m. writing notes during my 'evenings off'. I am not compelled to visit my patients in the evening for a chat; but such things are part of the caring by a GP for his patient.

Let me be more specific with a time-cost example. The other morning a farmer, John, gashed his leg, and Michael, a quarryman,

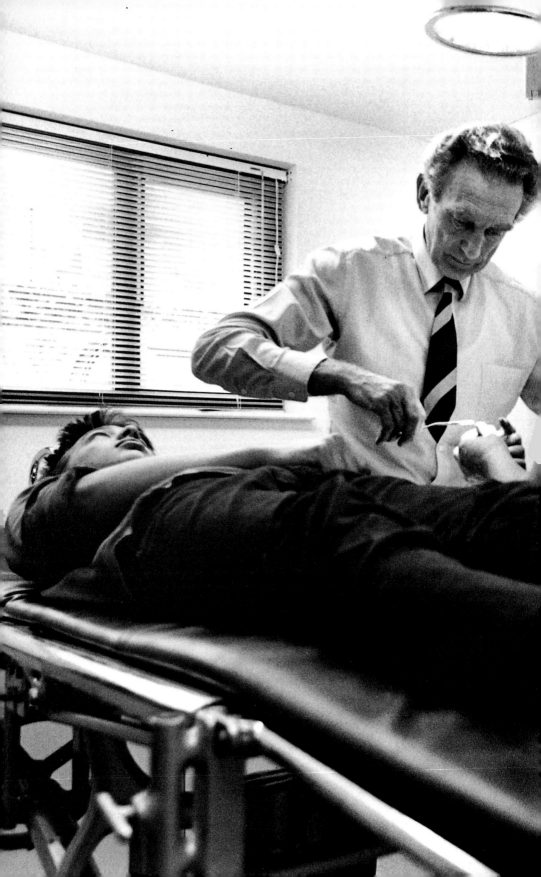

cut his forearm. Both arrived at the surgery for assessment and hopefully treatment. I was able to treat them both, and it took forty minutes out of my working day. In the morning I had to extend my surgery; in the afternoon curtail some of the paperwork at school surgery and start my evening surgery a bit late. Lunch or even a cup of tea were out the window. You never catch up.

Now I wasn't compelled to stitch either man. I might well have assessed and quite reasonably dispatched them to casualty at Airedale.

However, I knew Michael quite well – I've stitched him before; and I know what time is to a farmer like John, so I operated on both of them and they were quickly back to their respective jobs. Had I decided I wasn't prepared to 'waste' my time with them and dispatched them to hospital, each would have lost a minimum of a further two and a half hours out of their day; the NHS would have had to foot the bill for ambulances and the hospital casualty work itself. On the other hand I would not have lost forty minutes from my day and would probably have had time to grab some lunch, and I would not have gained or lost financially by either course of action. In the new climate driven by financial incentives, the doctor is bound to address himself to the question, 'Why bother?' This, for me, will be a tragedy.

The goodwill which I try to describe is the oil which lubricates the machinery of general practice administration. By its very nature it is probably immeasurable and certainly difficult to quantify. The story of Michael and John's stitches is just a small, but typical, example of it. But such goodwill permeates every corner of the job, and is just one of the things that makes the job so fascinating, so different and so exhausting. This raises the question of how a general practitioner can be assessed. Yardsticks of many kinds have been applied for this purpose many times, and increasingly frequently over the past few years. Knowledge of therapeutics or skills of technique may be assessed by examination and observation, but I doubt if skills such as the ability to communicate with patients under conditions which may vary from the happiest to the most tragic can ever be measured.

I PUT MY LETTER of resignation in a prominent place on my desk, in order to have a think about it for a while.

THURSDAY
5
APRIL

JUST AFTER I'D WALKED in from evening surgery tonight I had a call from Jane Caithness. Jane is the matron at the Prep School in Giggleswick, and though the school itself is on holiday, they're hosting a music course for about a hundred boys drawn from prep schools across the country. The Precentor of Eton College is leading them through Fauré's *Requiem* amongst other pieces, and I've been looking forward to the concert they're due to give at the end of the week.

Jane's problem tonight was rather unusual. Some of the boys have been suffering from peculiar rashes. Mysteriously the outbreak has been confined to one dormitory, and the top bunks at that.

The boys were in full voice, rehearsing in the music hall, and, as Jane and I approached, the *Requiem* floated towards us across the school quadrangle. In order not to disrupt the proceedings too much Jane signalled for one of the affected boys to come out to us. We took him into an adjoining instrument store room where we were surrounded by trombones and triangles and accompanied by music from the next room. I examined the offending red rash which the chorister declared was less itchy this evening. It didn't resemble any of the common infections which we were afraid of with such a large group of boys and we sent him back to join the others while we ran through possible causes.

The atypical nature of the rash, its marked short-lived itchiness and its limited distribution were altogether puzzling. We dismissed allergies to washing powder or food, since all the bedclothes had been washed together, and they all ate together. As we talked, something in the boy's description of the event sparked off an idea.

I thought back to my days in the very same school and the penny dropped. Itching powder. I well remembered the powerful red powder we used to send away for from adverts in the back of the *Beano* or some other comic.

We resolved to leave well alone and see if the rashes disappeared completely overnight.

I THEN DROVE out to Wigglesworth to see Willie Morphet. He's been out of Harden Bridge Hospital for a little over two weeks now, and his neighbour John Booth had phoned me to say he's not so good today. John told me Willie was a bit 'rutley' on his chest, a local word for congested. As I drove down the long track to his vast old farmhouse I knew I was not in for an easy time, because I expected to find a chest infection, and possibly a pneumonia. Willie has generally been getting very frail lately, and I knew the task tonight would not so much be dealing with the disease, as persuading him to go back to Harden Bridge.

To my annoyance when I went to open the door I found it locked. Looking at my watch I realised how stupid I'd been. It was only half past seven but Willie would have already been in bed for half an hour.

Walking around the corner to the Booths' bungalow I picked up a key from Freda. Standing in the last rays of the evening light, we discussed the chances of getting Willie into hospital again. Freda said he'd 'fair leapt home' from hospital two weeks ago, and he's since told her, 'I've come home to Wig to die.' At ninety-two years, I reckon that is probably his privilege, but it meant we were a few points down before we even started.

I took the key and we let ourselves in, through the old kitchen, down the darkened hallway into the front room where they'd put Willie's bed. I switched on the light, all 60 watts of it.

I could hear Willie before I could see him through the gloom. His breathing was pretty rough even at a distance of several feet.

'Now then, Willie, they tell me you're not so good again.' There was a slight stirring underneath the sheets, and after a cough a frail admission, 'No, I'm not so good.'

I put my bag down and sat by the bed.

'Do you feel hot?' I felt for his pulse as I waited for a reply.

'Yes, I'm a bit warm. I feel weak, you know what I mean.' He certainly looked a different person from the man who'd needed cajoling into having his broken arm X-rayed just a few weeks ago, indeed he seems to have been going downhill from that time.

Willie explained falteringly how he had started to cough the day after he'd come home from hospital, and it had just got worse. With John on the other side of the bed we lifted him up so I could listen to his chest.

There was no doubt of the diagnosis. Through the stethoscope

Opposite: Willie

I could hear the telltale rattle of the liquid in his lungs which indicated pneumonia. I told him about this infection in the right side of his chest. While not wishing ever to hide anything, I'm usually reluctant to use the word pneumonia to elderly patients. To some it has the same psychological effect as if they'd seen the Grim Reaper walk into the room.

We eased his hot body back down into the bed. Then came the difficult bit.

'What do you think we should do then, Willie?'

There was a long pause, filled only by the sound of the colony of rooks roosting in the trees beside the house and punctuated by Willie's wheezing.

His eyes moved slowly between the two of us. 'I don't know,' he said at last. 'No idea.'

'Well I have. But I'm sure you're not going to like it.'

I paused again to give him the opportunity to speak. He said nothing.

I tried again. 'Do you know what I'm going to say?'

'I'm not going away from here, Doctor,' he said without hesitation.

I knew we weren't going to get anywhere with him from that moment, but, equally, I knew I should try again.

'Well, who's going to nurse you?'

'Never mind. Somebody'll do it.' His voice became stronger each time he spoke.

'Well who? These boys are busy lambing, you know that.' I looked up to John who raised his eyebrows in defeat.

'Somebody'll do it!' he repeated.

I pressed on. 'You see if I can keep you warm and comfortable for two, maybe three, days, then we can get your chest better.'

Willie was getting into fighting mood now. 'I get bad chests and I get better. It'll be all right in a day or two.'

'Well, it's possible,' I said. 'But it'll be all right for sure if we can get you into Harden—' Willie cut me off with a wave of his hand.

'I'm not going into Harden Bridge. Not on no consideration.'

At least there was a spark in his eyes again now as he lay looking up at us. Then Willie's final thrust. 'I'm not open to argument!'

John smiled at the glimpse of the strong-minded, stubborn

man we both knew so well, and I capitulated.

I opened my bag to get him an injection of antibiotic. As we rolled him over on his side he let out what can only be described as a shriek. I wondered what had happened. 'What's up?'

'Your blimmin hands is cold!' he shrieked again. There was life in the old boy yet.

He gave another shriek well after the needle had been removed. 'Go on, you old soldier,' I said, smiling at John. 'You'll have done that to plenty of animals in your time, with colder hands than mine, Willie.'

He chuckled. 'I daresay I have.'

We straightened up the bed and I told him I'd call again to see him tomorrow.

In the murky, freezing front parlour on the other side of the hall, I asked John if Willie had any heating in his bedroom. John explained that he went around switching everything off to save electricity. We discussed the possible choices for looking after him in the future, of which the only viable one seems to be to find someone to live in the house and look after him. And who in this world would contemplate that; and anyway – as John commented – 'They wouldn't last long wi' Willie!' I knew there was no immediate answer to this problem, and that it was only the likes of Freda and John that could, and would, cope with him.

I went back to their house with John and told him and Freda again how I realised what a load it was for them, both the actual physical task and the responsibility. Neither of them are related to Willie; they just happen to live across the yard. On Monday Freda does get a half 'day off' when Mary Briggs, a remarkable lady herself in her seventies, comes across the valley from Long Preston to help Willie, as she has done for years. But I can imagine we'll have an even bigger fight with Willie to introduce any new help.

As I WALKED UP to the school chapel with Jane before the concert it was no great surprise to discover that the mysterious rashes had disappeared. The choir sang the Fauré *Requiem* without any surreptitious scratching in the pews, so presumably the culprit had either decided to stop his tricks or had run out of supplies!

I'm on call this weekend, so Scottie stayed at home in case there was a crash call, when she could whip up to the chapel and find me in my strategically placed seat. The school chapel is a wonderful setting for any music. Its acoustics are perfect for choral works, and the beautiful mosaics set into the dome are pleasing to the eye. The striking green of the weathered, copper-covered dome makes it a landmark for miles around, indeed many people mistake it for an observatory.

It was difficult for me to sit in the chapel listening to the music, without thinking back to the days when I occupied the same pews, but in short trousers. I came to Giggleswick School for the first time in 1942 as a day boy, my parents paying fees they could ill afford. They were more than a little concerned about my education and pushed me into a period of concentrated cramming following three years of war-enforced educational neglect.

There were no boarding places available, but my father was so anxious to get me into Giggleswick that he arranged digs with Miss Blanche Bentham at Mayville Terrace, Settle, not 100 yards from my present home.

I rode to school every day on my Raleigh bicycle, which I was only allowed to bring to the back gate of my digs where it was to be left outside the back door. My freedom of the house extended to just my small bedroom and brief periods in the kitchen for breakfast and supper which always left me hungry. Miss Bentham meant well, but I don't think she really understood how young growing boys needed to eat.

I found some consolation from the tiny dormer window of my bedroom, through which I could see the railway. I could lie in bed at night looking out at the embankment and watch the goods trains on the Settle to Carlisle line negotiate the famous long drag. On the way down the trains were stretched by applying the brakes on the guard's van at the rear. By the time the train passed my vantage point the van's chassis would be incandescent as a result of the immense friction, with sparks flying off the wheels. On the up line they put two engines at the front pulling, and a third behind pushing. The big quarry loads took a good deal of persuading to go up the incline, their wheels slipping and creating more sparks. All this from my bed was quite a thrill for a small boy, whose life held few other treats.

There was a great deal of bullying at school, and for the first couple of years at least it was fairly unpleasant for a scrawny lad who was a poor academic, a very moderate rugby player, but thankfully a better athlete.

As THE MUSIC from the concert in the school chapel washed over me this afternoon my thoughts drifted to the present. I'm now the school doctor and very much involved with health education as well as sickness and accidents.

It's a service for which the practice receives an extra payment because a good deal of my duties are outside the remit of the National Health Service. Our pupils come from all over the world, so the immunisation programme becomes a little involved with changing criteria and increasing demands. In addition to daily surgeries, every Tuesday morning at 8.15 a.m. I meet the Headmaster and drive him slowly up the hill to chapel. It gives us fifteen minutes to talk through any routine problems, before he has morning service and I dash back for the phone-in. Increasingly my role is becoming a pastoral one shared with Norman Daniels, the padre, who also helps with the health education programme – indeed he now teaches the major part of it. Norman and I are great friends and many a pupil's problem has been discussed over a glass of something medicinal in the late evening.

I ENJOY MY continuing contact with a school I'm proud to have attended, an involvement which was only continued after a long journey which brought me to my present medical role. My first recollection of any interest in medicine is of being intrigued by a book on human anatomy which I found in my father's library. It was the only medical volume in quite a large collection, and I can picture it vividly: a pink-covered tome which I would pore over for hours as a child, and through whose pages I became fascinated by the workings of the body. As I grew older my choice of career

in something biological seemed inevitable.

I was never an academic and as I struggled with Higher School Certificate through the long months of 1948 my call-up papers arrived as a welcome diversion, halting any move towards wearing a white coat, and requesting my appearance in khaki for King and Country. After being demobilised from the army early in 1950 I had the months leading up to the following autumn in which to pass a few exams in order to gain a university place. I looked around for something to do in the interim and ended up back at Giggleswick Prep School teaching, of all subjects, maths!

The teaching work at Giggleswick fitted in conveniently with my studies. We'd put the boys to bed by eight, have supper and a glass of beer, and I'd then have from nine o'clock onwards to study. Closeted in my little room in the total silence of the country I could really get some work done.

Despite my interest in the pink book in my father's library, I had dismissed any thoughts of reading medicine after a master at school told me I hadn't the academic ability. Looking back, this was a ridiculous thing to say to anyone, since it dampened my ardour and made me feel I had failed before I'd even started. Nevertheless I knew I wanted to become involved in a similar subject so I changed to Natural Sciences, specialising in marine zoology. At the time Trinity College, Dublin, had particular fame in this field, so that was where I set my sights. When I eventually took the entrance exams they were exactly the same as for medicine, as was the first year of the course! So I ended up studying identical material alongside the very people I had been told I could never match.

A FEW DAYS BEFORE term was due to start I arrived on Dublin's Westland Row station, feeling bloody lonely. I knew not a single person in Ireland, north or south.

I ended up in digs in a suburb of Dublin, in an old brick Victorian house with a big bay window, behind which was my big, cold room. My first term was miserable. I caught the bus into and out from college, worked hard, but had a pretty solitary time. Then of course I began to meet one or two people in the same situation. One of them was Denis Lockhart who was then in his first year of medicine. He and another guy called David Pim invited me to share their rooms in college, which made a heck of a difference. At last university life took a turn for the better.

The rooms were extraordinary, now I come to think of them. They were at the top of a three-storey building, up some creaky wooden steps. The facilities were spartan: one ceiling electric light, a single gas ring for cooking, and a jug and basin for washing in. There was no running water. The only tap, yielding icy cold water, was outside in the quadrangle about 30 yards away from our building.

Despite the Dickensian privations we still wore gowns for 'Commons', as the evening meal in college was called, and generally made hay.

Academic studies were seen largely as an unwelcome interruption to sport and the practical study of a particularly fine stout. The actual brand name was seldom used. An order of 'a pint' or 'a glass' proving sufficient to yield a pint or half respectively of the pure black and cream liquid produced by the descendants of Arthur Guinness, in a brewery not more than a mile away from the front gate of Trinity.

IT WAS A SPLENDID DECADE to be in Dublin, 1950–59, although I'm sure we didn't fully appreciate the many opportunities open to us. We drank jars with Brendan Behan in the Lincoln's Inn and often bumped into him about town; Michael MacLiammóir was playing at the Gate Theatre; Sean O'Casey's plays were being performed just by the side of College, and for sixpence you could get in to see *Juno and the Paycock*. Sadly, few of us medical students had the wit to take advantage of all that was on offer.

THE EXAMS WERE taken at a terrible time of year – after the summer break. Which meant you had to resist the many temptations of the summer to continue studying. I managed to do so and in September 1954 I qualified with a master's degree in marine zoology.

Like many young people I hadn't given much thought to what was next. I had my degree and a pink. At Oxford you get a blue, at Trinity it's a pink. If you went on to help promote sport for others once you'd received your pink you could become a Knight of the Campanile, named after the carved stone knights around the great bell tower in the middle of Front Square, something which I was lucky enough to do.

So when someone planted the idea of going to Oxford to try for a blue in athletics, it was appealing. Since I'd already experienced a short spell of teaching, and was assured that a diploma in education would be a useful idea, I went up to Oriel College, Oxford. My main ambitions while I was there were to learn to fly and get my blue. I knew quite a few athletes at Oxford by this time and everything seemed fairly laid on.

On my first night, after I'd settled into my digs, I found myself in the gardens walking round and round a tree. I can see it now – I must have been there for several hours. I felt very torn and unsure. Just before I'd left Dublin I had been offered a place back at Trinity to read medicine. Until then I'd really dismissed it as a serious possibility, since I'd been told at school that I wasn't up to it.

I found myself nearly pulled in two by the decision. Should I stay and learn to fly and win my blue, or go back and study medicine which had always been my ambition.

After a few tortuous days of thought I went to see my tutor, a Dr Turner. We had a couple of glasses of sherry and talked for over an hour, at the end of which he said, 'Well, what do you really want to do?' When I replied, 'Medicine,' he urged me, 'Well for heaven's sake, man, go and do it!' I'm not sure if it was the worst or best advice I've ever had, but I suppose it was fairly sound.

ON THE WAY BACK to Trinity I had to sort out my family's reactions. Having hitchhiked up the A1 towards Leeds, I walked up the road to my home where I could see my father digging in the garden. He looked up and saw me; surprise flickered across his face, then concern.

I broke the news. 'Dad, I'm going back to Trinity to study medicine.' He looked at me for a moment, put the spade back in the earth, turned another shovelful of soil, and said gently in his warm Yorkshire accent, 'Go inside. Your mother will want to put the kettle on. I'll join you in a moment.'

No histrionics or anger. No problems at all, even though he knew straight away it would mean another five years of dependence on him in some way or other. I made it clear later in the evening that I would try and work my way through medical school.

I have always treasured that example of love and support.

I RETURNED TO Trinity and walked into the first year of what was to become my medical life. Everything was going well until just into my second year I noticed I hadn't been doing very well in my athletic activities, with my lap times falling off a bit. I was screened, only to discover I had pulmonary tuberculosis. I rushed back to Yorkshire where the diagnosis was confirmed, and I was admitted forthwith to Killingbeck hospital.

At first, this seemed like a real setback, since I was to be forced to lie on my back for six months, and I wondered if it would be the end of my medical life. I soon came to realise that it could provide a much-needed bonus, because at the end of the second medical year the feared 'Half' exams loomed. They were a tough set of papers in anatomy, physiology and chemistry which many a candidate has sat more than once.

However, lying on my back I had nothing to do but read. My father fixed up a tilting table which could take the weight of such massive tomes as Gray's *Anatomy,* Grant's *Atlas of Anatomy* and those huge physiology books. So I spent most of my time studying.

I remember those six months at Killingbeck vividly. There were seventeen guests of D wing, the other sixteen all men over fifty. I was put in an octagonal side ward so I could study, away from the cacophony of productive coughing which emerged from my fellow inmates.

There was a large nurse who we nicknamed 'The Butcher'. The Butcher used to come round every day with a large trolley full of her implements of torture: syringes, each of which carried a gram of Streptomycin. Despite her multiple and daily practice on the equivalent of about fifty backsides, she had the worst technique of injection ever: slow, hesitant, uncertain, messy, and therefore not surprisingly painful for the recipient. I sometimes picture her now when syringe and needle are in my hand and hope my technique has borrowed nothing from hers.

The Superintendent of this special lung and chest unit was Dr Gilmour, a wonderful man who wandered around the hospital with his entourage of sisters and doctors, always wearing sandals and smoking Woodbine cigarettes out of the corner of his mouth in a short yellow alabaster holder. He may not have epitomised the expected image of a hospital superintendent, but he was a natural leader of men.

One morning, during non-visiting hours, Sister put her head

round my door and said I had a party of rather more than the permissible number of visitors; she gave me a wicked wink and in walked the Trinity Rugby team led by Huby O'Connor – the boys were over the water playing Headingley. It was a moment to be savoured during my solitary confinement.

When I returned to Dublin to take the exams, I found I'd worked harder than anyone else, purely through my enforced solitude. So with an exam pass to my credit I resumed athletics training and some old acquaintances in the Lincoln's Inn and Jammet's back bar. More importantly, I was back in Dublin for the start of our clinical year and attended Sir Patrick Dunn's Hospital, or Paddy Dunn's as we called it. These were to be tough but happy years.

INTERESTING PEOPLE were still about. Brendan Behan was still alive, still brilliant, and still drunk. Liam O'Flaherty was still sitting in the Burlington Bar, being pleasant or unpleasant. I think he sometimes got himself screwed up trying to be both at the same time. Paddy Kavanagh continued to walk up and down the north side of Pembroke Road just outside our flat, his hands thrust deep up the sleeves of his great long Crombie overcoat, reciting his poetry. Ulick O'Connor still told some of the funniest and rudest stories I've ever heard, and all on just ginger ale or orange juice. In between he'd wander off and break the Irish pole vault record or write another book.

AS RESIDENT medical students in our house year we had periods where we lived and worked in the hospital twenty-four hours a day. It was a good way of learning. We worked all the time available for little recompense. The twelve pounds a month we did receive went straight into the till of Burke's pub about five doors down from the hospital, to help wipe a little more from the slate. I wonder if I ever succeeded in paying it off completely?

At Paddy Dunn's we were privileged to study under several great clinicians. Jackie Wallis and Heber McMahon were two of them. At one of Jackie Wallis's clinics he took us to examine a sailor who had obviously survived time at sea during the First World War judging by the tattoos on his arms, and also appeared to have sworn his undying love to a range of ladies, from Ada to Violet, in variously coloured dyes. He had come in suffering from symptoms associated with an aneurysm of the aorta, a sort of spindle-shaped enlargement of the main artery from the heart, and Jackie asked us for observations as to the possible causes.

We all offered our various suggestions, some ridiculous, some clever, but all obviously wrong judging by our tutor's wincing eyebrows. After we ran out of suggestions he said, 'Gentlemen, look at the patient's arms. Note the tattoos and read the story they tell.' We clambered around the chap, subjecting the works of art to close scrutiny, in the expectation of discovering some local lesion caused by the tattooing.

Pointing to the etchings of destroyers, Jackie said that we obviously all recognised this brave man's outstanding war record.

'But, gentlemen, whilst appreciating the wars of Mars,' he intoned as he moved his finger to one of the more lascivious tattoos, 'remember also the wars of Venus.'

The light dawned. The patient's problems were caused by syphilis, no doubt contracted as a result of one of his many amorous encounters with girls from around the world, some of whom were now listed for posterity on his body. A diagnosis was reached, but far more importantly the process of reasoned observation had been demonstrated.

By an amazing fluke I never failed an exam in all my time at Trinity and duly qualified, albeit after a struggle, in 1959. During my time there I'd had little time for the Territorial Army, except for one short period when I was inveigled into helping out at a camp with the 12/13th Parachute Regiment by a good friend, Larry L'Estrange. It poured with rain incessantly and one wet, miserable evening sitting in a sodden tent with another platoon commander, Stephen Fox, we hatched a plot which was to take us around the world. Our plan was to acquire a Landrover or two, and disappear around the globe for a year.

I still had a year's medicine to do, so I tried to qualify while Stephen did much of the work of administration and preparation to get the expedition together. Eventually we assembled a group of eight from the battalion, from window cleaners through ship-wrights to electrical engineers. We drew maps of the world on our Landrover doors, and called ourselves 'Pegasus Overland' after the flying Pegasus emblem of the Parachute Regiment.

We trundled off on 10 December 1959, to motor across Europe through Asia to the Far East.

FROM SINGAPORE we sailed for North-west Australia, camping out on the cattle decks of our ship. We docked at a place in the north-west called Derby and disembarked. This was just as well because thousands of cattle got on.

We had no more than £16 between us, and had to find work to make enough money to finance our return home. Having just qualified as a doctor I set about looking for a medical job in order to gain more experience. My only hope was to register in Perth by presenting my credentials in person to some bureaucrat at the department of health, in order to work in one of the city's hospitals. So I made my way there and turned up at Fremantle Hospital where I was ushered in to see a guy called John Rowe. He was the superintendent of the hospital and to my relief and joy he hired me.

In three months there I learnt more about surgery and medicine than I did in nine months in the UK. You just had to get on with it. There was an ENT surgeon, an archetypal bronzed Australian called Frankie Farmer who had a great way of sharing his skills. We were in theatre one day when he suddenly looked up from his scalpel and asked, 'Here, Barry, you ever taken out any tonsils?' I replied that I'd hardly even looked down a throat.

The next day in theatre he returned to his theme. 'This is how it's done.' I concentrated fiercely on his moves, which he performed at incredible speed and with amazing deftness, humming all the time. Then as the patient was being wheeled out and the next brought in, he placed the instruments in my hand and said, 'It's your go, mate.'

I started dissecting away very slowly and rather nervously. After a few minutes I came to a stage where I wasn't sure of the next move. Still hunched over the table I asked, 'Do you go to the left or the right down here?'

No answer. I looked up and around and he'd disappeared. I was on my own, there was no choice but to carry on. It took me about forty minutes to dissect that particular pair of tonsils, as opposed to the ten he'd been taking to whip them out. The anaesthetist was very tolerant, if restless, and the next set came out in twenty minutes. A few sets later I was on a par with Frankie.

By the end of the three months I'd done a fair amount of surgery and masses of casualty work. I almost got the itch to carry on with surgery, but I wasn't sure I could have flogged away at the necessary fellowship examinations. However by the time I left I felt more like a real doctor.

The social life was lived at much the same pace as the surgery, and was equally interesting and rewarding. I returned to my room in hospital early one morning, I suspect after seeing a young lady, and climbed into my bedroom through the French windows which were always left open on account of the temperature. Being hospital-made beds, the top sheet was always tucked in very tightly which I hated, so every time before I climbed into bed I was in the habit of pulling the sheet off to loosen it and simply laying it back over the top. On this particular night my colleagues had obviously planned a surprise for me. However they were unaware of my nocturnal habit of stripping the bed before retiring. As I pulled back the crisp white sheet, an unwelcome guest in my sleeping quarters was revealed. He was shiny, filled most of the bed and flapped: a huge skate had been planted there to await my return, and the poor creature was literally taking its last gasp as I came upon it.

Deciding to exact immediate revenge, I opened my door and crept out into the subdued nighttime light of the hospital corridor. My room was only a few yards from the entrance to the operating theatre, where the trolleys were in line awaiting the following day's patients. Temptingly, they were complete with their neatly laundered linen ready to be wheeled to the wards to collect the patients for theatre.

I must have overslept the next morning because I was cruelly awoken by female screams. In my semi-conscious state I rushed to the door and flung it open to see a screaming nurse backed against the wall, recoiling from a trolley whose sheet had slipped off to reveal the massive form of a still shiny, but thankfully very dead skate.

MY TIME AT THE Fremantle came to an end all too soon and I was reluctant to leave. If it hadn't been for loyalty to the expedition I might well have remained there to this day. However, at the outset of Pegasus Overland we'd made two agreements between ourselves: whatever happened we would return to England with the two Landrovers, and we would return together. No excuses would be accepted for breaking either of these bonds.

Largely because of this attitude of strict adherence to our agreement, one week less than a year after setting out those two criteria were fulfilled. We drove into Turks Row, the paras' HQ in London, where we were welcomed by quite a party including my proud father.

ON RETURN TO ENGLAND I had to get down to some medicine, having completed only three months' house officer work in Fremantle. I was qualified, of course, but had another nine months' house officer work to complete my training.

I managed to get a job in the Adelaide Hospital in Dublin doing an orthopaedic job under a great man called Sean Sugars. On my first operating day I was attempting to scrub up using the normal elbow tap handles, but couldn't make them work. I turned to a rather lovely looking nurse wearing one of the somewhat diaphanous cotton theatre gowns and asked, 'How the bloody hell do you work these things!'

She turned deftly, distracting my attention by looking me straight in the eyes, firmly placed her foot on the newly installed foot tap and nearly drowned me. Those immortal first words will hardly go down in the annals of courtship as the most romantic opening lines, but they were my first to Scottie.

Cupid, or the hospital administrators, threw us together again that same evening, during night duty. A Catholic priest who had fallen off his bicycle was brought in to us by a National Fire Brigade ambulance because we were the nearest hospital. Although he was half conscious when we got to him, all he was concerned about was whether he was in a 'mick or a prot' hospital. I remember being severe with him and arguing with some feeling that it didn't matter as long as he got help. With Scottie's assistance I stitched up some nasty lacerations to his face. Despite the unromantic nature of this second encounter we saw more of each other from then on.

After some six months doing bones, then medicine and some ENT work, I had moved across to the Rotunda Hospital to

Opposite: Scottie

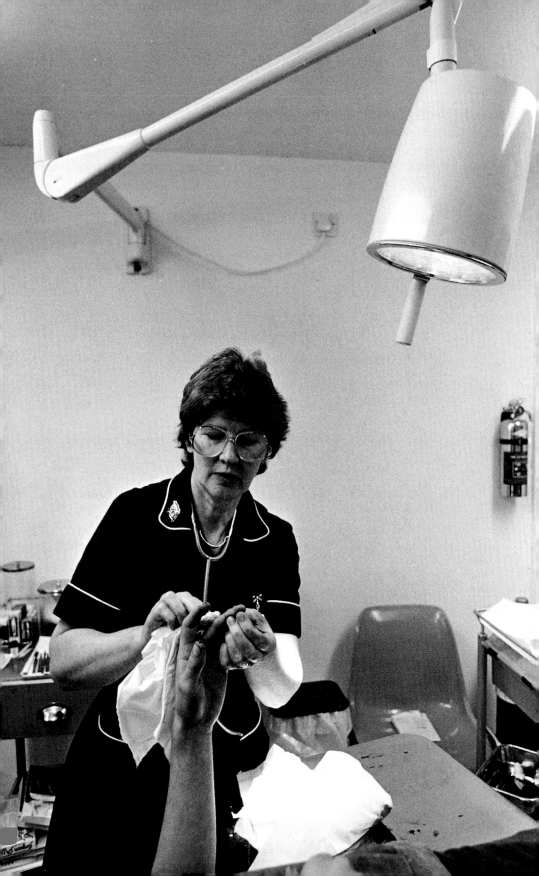

complete my training in gynaecology and obstetrics. At the Rotunda there was a great team: Huby O'Conner and Jimmy McGrath (now obstetricians), and Jimmy Lee (now a GP in Drogheda), amongst others. We were seldom off duty. If we wanted time off we got someone to cover for us. On the other hand this was largely to our advantage, after all if you're not there you can't learn. There was a bell system which sounded all over the hospital and whenever there was an interesting obstetric happening in the labour ward the alarm would sound and we would run for the ward whatever we were doing. There wasn't a bell in our favourite watering hole, Conway's, but the hospital porters who inhabited a lodge just across the road could be called upon to relay the alarm.

Once we were considered to have gathered enough knowledge, or be brave enough, we were assigned to what might now be thought of as an obstetric flying squad, but what we simply called 'being on the district'. The district was manned by two interns, which in my turn meant Jimmy Lee and me. We used to travel around the less salubrious areas of Dublin, to the many A/Bs (Abnormal Births), in an old VW ambulance.

We were called to rather a lot of 'mysterious' miscarriages in those days, but there had to be some answer to repeated pregnancies in Catholic families. Working in pairs, we'd be called out some time after the woman had started miscarrying and there would be no option but to complete the process with a dilatation and curettage (or D and C). It was fairly routine to do several of these cases in a night, mostly in the very poor areas of depressing tenement blocks. We'd put brown paper down on the bed, lie the woman across it on her back with her bottom sticking out over the edge and a zinc bath beneath to catch the bits. Jimmy and I worked as a pair and could read each other intuitively, which was a great boon at this particular stage of training. He would pour the ether on to the gauze mask to anaesthetise the patient while I performed the D and C. If we hadn't had the right attitude it could have become extremely depressing, but fortunately Jimmy was always good for a laugh to lighten things. I think there was only one occasion when I saw him without a smile on his face.

It was in a typical poor run-down tenement block on a bitter winter's night. We'd set everything up. The woman was lying across the bed and we were well under way, with Jimmy pouring the ether from the bottle on to the gauze mask. His task required concentration and skill to judge the amount used so as not to induce coughing or vomiting. Our patient was settling down nicely.

It was common on these occasions for a group of women, grandmothers, aunts or just neighbours, to gather in the kitchen with their black shawls wrapped around them, reminiscent of the ardent knitters at the guillotine. This night was no different, except colder. The sound of three or four old ladies in the next room talking in their strong Dublin accents was clearly audible to us as they discussed how they had found themselves in similar predicaments in days past.

In the middle of it all I heard the bedroom door open behind me. I glanced at Jimmy, only to see his face freeze in a terrified stare over my shoulder. When I turned I was confronted with one of the black attired old crones carrying a coal shovel full of glowing red cinders from the kitchen fire. 'I t'ought you might be cold, now, sir,' she said in her strong Dublin accent, 'so I brought t'ese coals in from t'kitchen.'

Jimmy was speechless, all he could do was look from the open bottle of highly volatile and inflammable ether in his hand to the old woman as she advanced purposefully across the room towards the fireplace next to him. For a moment I wondered if he was going to throw the bottle away from him in sheer panic. Very gently I croaked, not wanting to induce any sudden movement of the shovel, 'Now that's terrible kind of you, Mam, but we're sweating in here. Please, please (God!), take the coals back to the kitchen and we'll join you for a mug of tea in a minute.'

She left and Jimmy's knuckles slowly turned from white back to pink as his grasp on the ether bottle softened. 'It's more than bloody tea I'll be havin' after that,' he breathed.

As MY TIME at the Rotunda was coming to an end, my grandfather, of whom I was very fond, fell and broke his leg. I got the boat from Dublin to the Liver Buildings, a 19a Kirby tram to the East Lancs road from where I hitchhiked home to Leeds – this way I often beat the train from Lime Street station.

While I was there the phone rang and it was Mr Dutton, from Giggleswick School. He asked if anyone in the house knew where I was. When I told him it was me speaking he couldn't believe the coincidence. He'd been ringing to let me know there was a general practice in Settle which needed another partner, and wondered if I would be interested. It was a family of doctors called Hyslop, father and two sons. One of the sons, Tony, had suddenly decided to pack up and leave for Canada.

Old Doctor Hyslop used to look after Giggleswick School when I was a boy there. A great figure: terrific fisherman, terrible driver, who always urged his car around in top gear and used the clutch for control. He was well retired, so with his brother off to Canada too, the second son, David, was looking for a partner urgently.

I told Mr Dutton I'd come and look, but it was more out of respect for him than a genuine interest in general practice. As house doctors we just about knew what GPs were, but little else. Our main impression of them was formed by the blacklist we had pinned to the mantelpiece in the hospital mess. When a GP rang up on a Friday night asking for a patient to be admitted for the weekend we looked at the list and if he was on it we said: 'Sorry, no beds.' We knew that the blacklisted doctors did this to get rid of their problem patients in time for a quiet weekend.

Rather reluctantly I traipsed across Yorkshire, had a look at the practice and to my surprise found it interesting. However up to that point I'd been delivering dozens of babies at the Rotunda, and taking a postgraduate degree in midwifery which I was determined to finish.

I told David Hyslop, my prospective senior partner, that I'd love to join him but wouldn't be able to do so for about nine months, the remaining time of my postgraduate course. In those days there was a shortage of locums to cover even for a holiday, let alone nine months, so it was as good as saying no.

I was back in Dublin with the lads telling this story when another medic, Ted Nolan, joined us and listened to the end of the tale. 'Hang on a minute,' he said. 'My father retired from the army eighteen months ago and has got itchy feet. I think he'd leap at the chance of a locum for a year in the country.'

He did, and held the fort while I finished my postgraduate course. In his short time in the district he became a well-known figure. I'm sure his black labrador went into just about every house in Settle.

Suddenly I found myself at the end of my course. There I

was one morning in the Rotunda, looking anxiously at my wallet to see how many pound notes I had left; the next I was in Settle having bought a house for thousands of pounds I didn't have. I had to buy it because it contained the surgery and waiting room, but at the time everyone thought I was mad to borrow so much money. It is the house we still live in today.

THE CONCERT CAME to an end, and I slipped out before the mass of parents' cars clogged up the road. Just as I walked in the door at home the phone went. Spiritually refreshed, I felt ready to deal with anything, even a woman who'd somehow dropped a wardrobe on her big toe. The *Requiem* will still be listened to with wonder in a thousand years, but large wardrobes and big toes will be long forgotten.

Overleaf: Sunday morning

ALTHOUGH I'VE BEEN on duty this weekend I've been trying to catch up on my gardening in between calls. It's usually an erratic process; the phone always seems to ring just as I'm about to sow a row of seeds, or transplant some seedlings which have been nurtured in, or rather survived, my greenhouse. This tends to be drowned one end of the week, only to be left parched for the rest.

This morning's efforts were no exception. Under a clear blue sky, with just a gentle breeze to make the work more pleasant, I'd dug a trench the full width of the garden, and was feeling hopeful that at last I was about to sow my broad beans. The ring of the cordless phone strapped to my waist shattered those hopes.

In a thin, distressed voice Peter explained that he'd been vomiting for two days and wasn't feeling too good. From the sound of him, that was an understatement.

Peter is a diabetic and that knowledge, added to his description of his state, was enough for me to realise that I needed to get over to his home in Giggleswick fairly quickly, on the way radioing ambulance control to put a van on standby.

Peter was lying in bed in a semi-comatose state. There were signs of his vomiting all around the room, mostly stained with old dark blood. As I opened my bag and took out my stethoscope I asked him how long he'd been like he was.

In his dream-like state he told me he'd been ill for two days. We were interrupted by the ring of the phone by his bedside. I answered saying that it was Dr Brewster, thinking it might be Scottie or the ambulance control with another call-out. It was Peter's mother wanting to know where he was, since he was supposed to be with her for Sunday lunch. I explained that Peter was not quite so well and that I'd phone her later.

I tried again to get Peter, in his confused state, to tell me more about what had happened. 'I want a drink,' he kept saying. I told him he would be getting some fluid soon. 'And you know where as well, don't you! In hospital.'

He didn't answer, but lay there with his eyes closed, sighing. Moments later he managed to tell me that he'd not eaten for two days, and that it had got worse over the last twenty-four hours.

'Why didn't you let me know before, you crazy bugger!'

'I didn't want to be a fuss, and usually I get over it. . . .' His voice trailed off. The effort of speaking was too much.

I asked if he knew of anything that might have started his vomiting. He shook his head.

I checked his blood pressure which was slightly low, though his pulse was fast and thready; then I took some blood from a vein in his arm.

'When did you last check your blood sugar?'

'Two days ago,' he murmured.

I was finding it difficult to control my temper. Most diabetics are sensible about looking after themselves, as Peter usually is. But it's peculiar how we can all be negligent about our own health and illnesses. He knew from my voice what I was thinking because he ventured the comment, 'I'm a pillock, aren't I?'

I couldn't help laughing at his realisation of his own stupidity. He is a likeable chap and right now needed encouragement.

'Oh for a really good pint,' he licked his lips at the thought.

'You'd like to come down to *The Old Station*?' I suggested.

Peter smiled, but he was obviously feeling the strain of the last couple of days.

'Can I have a drink, Barry?' he asked again.

I told him I didn't think it a good idea, since it would just make him puke again. I placed a drop of blood on the special receptor card of the glucometer, a machine which looks like a pen with a hole for the card at one end and a digital readout of the blood sugar level on the other. In order to read it I held it under his bedside light, over an ashtray full of cigarette ends.

'I should have removed those fag ends,' muttered Peter, glancing at the table through one eye which he'd cranked open in one of his more lucid moments.

'Yes, that's something else we won't talk about, Peter.'

As expected, the reading was high, confirming that Peter might be heading for a diabetic coma. Not surprising since he hadn't eaten or drunk anything for a couple of days, and he'd been vomiting pretty frequently.

'Well, lad, we're going to have to get you in.'

'Oh hell!' was Peter's only response. I think he'd been hoping we'd be able to cope with things there. What he needed, as he'd said himself, was fluid, but not from one of Mr Joshua Tetley's hostelries. The place to get it was Airedale Hospital, and with the ambulance virtually at the door I dismissed the idea of putting up a saline drip myself.

The first thing he'd receive in hospital would be fluid by intravenous drip, which would reduce the amount of insulin required to lessen the excessive circulating blood sugar. I radioed ambulance control and confirmed I needed the van.

When the ambulance lads arrived they announced they'd brought another patient with them, having been at a road traffic accident when my warning call had come over the radio. In the back of the van was a man who'd injured his arm in the collision and while they were managing Peter down the stairs they asked me to have a look at their other customer.

His elbow was swollen, and he described a tingling sensation in his fingers. On examination he had a cold hand and pain around the elbow when he attempted to move it. It looked as though it was broken, by virtue of the position, the swelling and the loss of function. Nor did I like the cold hand and tingling – it might mean that there had been some damage to the nerve as it tracked around the bony prominences of the elbow joint, and that would be bad news for the chap.

There wasn't much I could do except tell the lads to put a sling around it to take the weight off the joint and give him some Entonox if he needed it. This is modern laughing gas which temporarily relieves pain, without spoiling the clinical picture for the orthopaedic boys when the patient gets to casualty.

Peter was stretchered into the ambulance and settled down on his side. I went back to telephone the hospital as it drove off.

As I was leaving, his sister came along and I explained the situation to her, asking her to pass on the news gently and diplomatically to their mother.

'I'm sure he'll be all right once his dehydration has been dealt with and they've given him the right amount of insulin.

There's a navigational flag which indicates that a boat is 'steaming into danger' and Peter should have been flying it. Everything had happened slowly at first, like a boat getting nearer to another vessel, then, because he did nothing to avert the problem, it suddenly became serious. I think he'll have learned a lesson from the experience.

It was time to get back to my broad beans.

I DROVE OUT TO Willie Morphet's farm today, to see how he's recovering from his pneumonia. With the roof off the car, Louis Armstrong singing my favourite 'What a wonderful world' from the cassette machine and the sun beating down, the drive to the farm was invigorating.

As I drove along the track leading to the house I had to wait while a breakaway group of sheep took their time to amble across my path. On a rainy day I might well have become frustrated at the delay; today I was content to sit it out and take my turn.

Freda Booth stopped washing the dishes as I went into the kitchen and told me she thought Willie was worse. She explained that he'd fallen yesterday when he'd tried to get to the window, and was obviously weak.

In Willie's front room Freda's teenage daughter, Helen, was sitting on the bed holding his lunch plate. The sunlight streaming through the windows made the place less forbidding than it had seemed a few days ago under the light of the single 60 watt bulb.

Willie was sitting up in bed chewing slowly, and he explained he was having problems swallowing. 'It just goes round and round!' he said in exasperation, his scrawny hands describing a circle on the bedspread. I tried to get him to have a drink to help it down, but it didn't seem to make much difference. He took a pathetic few drops from the glass offered by Helen.

'I've seen you drink more than that in your time, Willie!' He laughed, and that was an important and encouraging sign.

When he'd finished eating as much as he could manage, I listened to his chest. I was pleasantly surprised to hear it less rutley than before; the antibiotics were obviously winning their battle.

I gave him another injection which was an event in its own right. We went through the same, 'Your hands is cold,' routine and he offered an even more virulent objection to the needle than last time.

My ministrations complete, I spoke to Freda back out in the kitchen and I told her I was pleased with his progress, but asked her to try and get him to drink more if possible. Young Helen, who has obviously been playing her part in his recovery, explained that he'd had some tea earlier on. The Booths have been consistently good to him, but he's a stubborn old bugger and he'll do things in his own time as he wants to.

It must be some eight years since Willie's wife Ann died. She was a fine woman who latterly got dreadful arthritis and was confined to the house except when Willie took her out which, I'm afraid, wasn't very often. She used to sit in the room where Willie now lies in bed, and watch television or listen to the wireless. One morning I called in and was pretty aghast to find her so immobile, and straining her eyes to watch a tiny black and white TV screen with a snowy picture you could hardly see. I told her that she ought to get a decent sized colour television so at least she'd have the pleasure of that to help her during her incapacity. Ann's comment was, 'Well, you'll have a job getting one out of Willie.'

At that moment Willie chanced to return in his Landrover and came shuffling in the back door, so I whipped out into the kitchen and told him I'd had a brilliant idea. 'You know you like your football, Willie?'

'Oh aye.'

'Well I've just come from a farm down the road where they were watching a match on a colour set and it looks marvellous. It'd really improve your enjoyment of the game.'

'I think we'll manage on with the one we've got.' It was a pretty definite answer.

Not to be beaten, I asked him the name of his television dealer, and he told me it was Slatterys' in Skipton. Armed with this information I said I'd bet him a fiver that if I got one in for him he'd be so impressed he'd not send it back. Willie couldn't resist the possibility of making five pounds and was obviously convinced that he would return it as soon as it arrived. His only comment was, 'Nay, but a fiver's not so much.'

I used Willie's own telephone, which made him wince a bit, and I did a deal with a man at Slattery's who knew the ropes, and Willie. I told him I wanted him to get a colour TV out to Wig Hall and working by four o'clock that same afternoon.

To give the man his due, it was in and working by three o'clock. I said nothing for a few days, after which it became unnecessary to ask who'd won the bet. Willie was delighted with

Opposite:
Wigglesworth Hall, Willie's home

the new addition, despite losing out on his fiver, and I was equally pleased that at least Ann sitting there with her painful rheumatism had a decent picture to watch. I never did get my fiver.

Now Willie lies in the same bed and watches his snooker and his football on the same set. He could really do with a remote control to make his life easier, but I don't think I'll push my luck.

'I'll make do,' must be Willie's favourite expression, indeed he used it again on me last week. His ceiling light fitting takes three bulbs, but there sat Willie reading the paper by just one – all 60 watts of it. It was casting no light on the paper and must have been a terrible strain on his eyes. I told him he really must get a small light above and behind the bed-head so he'd be able to read more easily.

Willie would have none of it; you'd think I'd suggested he floodlit the whole farm. Even when I tried to point out that this reading light would only need to hold a 40 watt bulb, and therefore might conceivably save him money, he still wouldn't listen. So I told him I would get one installed, which really made him cuss. 'It won't look right!' he said in a tone of finality. 'Anyway I won't be around long enough to get the benefit.' This was the ultimate justification for not running to such expense. So I left it. But I'll get something sorted out for the old begger one way or another.

I must also attempt to get Freda some financial reward for all the caring she's doing now and has done over the past few months. It's no good asking Willie, so I'll have to make approaches to his relatives.

Willie's case isn't the first time I've had to broach the issues of finance and fairness for such long-term care. It's always a difficult area, with a lot of thin ice about, but occasionally the doctor is the only one who can and must risk skating upon it.

MY LETTER OF RESIGNATION from the Conservative Association has been on my desk for a month now, while I gave myself time to think things over. My feelings about the new contract and the White Paper are unchanged, however, and it is about time I took the bit between my teeth and sent it off.

The 'new contract' was enforced upon GPs on 1 April this year 1990 and was not a contract, because by definition a contract is agreed by the two parties concerned, and there is little agreement here. The proposals made in the White Paper on health, which deal more with the overall intentions of the government concerning health care, are undergoing a process of introduction, and will not become law until a year after the GP contract. In the meantime, however, the White Paper provides an unhealthy smokescreen for the government's outflanking manoeuvre in the attack on general practice. Using the contract as their weapon, the objective of this attack was to improve those areas of poor general practice and inefficient health care delivery. But the details of the campaign were so badly thought out that much of good general practice was badly mauled while much of poor practice was left unmolested.

For years I have been working hard to improve the service we supply to our patients. Indeed in the decade up to 1990 our practice had been voluntarily evolving precisely in the way in which the White Paper and contract now seek to direct by enforcement. But there's an important distinction: willing and natural evolution is so much more motivated and healthy than compelled changes forced by a superior power – particularly when that power has little or no experience of the good work of general practice. For the many actively evolving practices like ours, the timing of the government's impositions is a tragedy, and has wrecked much of the carefully developing improvement in services to patients, and demoralised practice staff and GPs alike.

THE FAULTS ARE LARGELY in the carrot and stick methods of payment which the new contract uses in seeking to improve GPs' work.

A family doctor's pay is made up of three main parts: a salary, called the basic practice allowance; some particular fees for specific tasks that doctors carry out, such as night visits; and thirdly the capitation fee, that is the payment made per patient on the doctor's list.

A high proportion of the less effective general practices are in urban areas, with big lists of up to 3500 patients per doctor. The new contract increased the payment per patient by 14 per cent. Consequently, such practices have been given a rise of 14 per cent on their main factor of payment without lifting a finger. At the same time the relatively small sums of money paid for immunisation, cervical cytology and the like have become more difficult to obtain because of the higher targets necessary. So these large, less caring practices which the contract aimed to improve can accept their rise for nothing and care less for their patients, and in economic terms who can blame them.

In Settle we have no choice in the matter. As in many other rural areas, our style and size of practice, by virtue of its small list and patient-personal relationships, will be particularly affected by the new financial systems, despite our trained staff, computers, and past years of work towards better primary care. Our problem is that topographically we are almost an island, and our area is over 300 square miles. Our population is contained in over forty-eight hamlets and villages scattered throughout this hill and fell landscape. The roads radiate out from Settle like the points of a star, so that it is mostly necessary to return to the centre before going out to another call on the periphery. Because of the time this involves we couldn't cope with a list of many more patients, even if there were any more potential patients in the hills – which there aren't, just sheep.

Therefore small-list and rural practices can only look to maximise their income by persuading target percentages of their patients to undergo certain procedures, such as immunisation or cervical cytology. This has now been made more difficult to achieve. If we can persuade 50 per cent of our women patients between twenty and sixty-five years of age to undergo examination of their vaginas so that we can take smears from their cervices, then the practice is paid £734. If we can persuade another 29 per cent of our patients to have this done, we receive no further payment. One more vaginal examination, however, will attain our 80% target and bring the practice another £1,468. I sometimes wonder if we should give that particular lady a gold-plated model of a cervix as she leaves the surgery to thank her for her trouble.

What a way to run a Health Service!

There have already been charges of coercion, or over-enthusiastic persuasion of women to attend for smear tests. In some areas doctors have removed women from their lists because their non-attendance for smear tests threatened the attainment of targets. The fact that some women (for example, a woman who has been sexually abused) may not wish to attend for an internal examination seems of little concern to the authors of the new contract. What can this sort of thing do to relationships between the doctor and patient, even the lady with the gold-plated cervix?

Only the other day, Darren, who was just five months old, left our surgery in his mother's arms having just completed his inoculations. At that young age he had just earned the practice £1737, because he had brought us to our target figure of 90 per cent by his attendance. Without him we would have received only £579. If we had known we wouldn't attain the higher target there would have been no *financial* incentive to continue encouraging people to use the service, and some doctors will certainly stop when they know they have reached first base.

Of course, business methods and business efficiency must be applied to the administrative sections of general practice. Our own practice welcomes accountability or external audit – indeed we have undergone six external audits, and all of these were done in years well preceding the compilation of the contract or White Paper. But not all parts of family medicine are appropriate for business methods. People who promote health care require some security in order to carry through their tasks without the pressures of profit and loss. Health care is not a business, and it is not appropriate to apply business methods to its promotion in general practice.

Over the last eight years we, like many practices, have run clinics associated with things such as diabetes, hypertension, smoking and diet. We host visiting consultants, and run group meetings on asthma and sports injuries. In our own Well Person Clinic we have tried to educate people to adopt healthier lifestyles. It seems sensible to try and prevent people developing nasty

*Overleaf: A consultation which saved
Pat McEvoy removing his boots*

diseases, rather than just treating illnesses as they arise. We had a two-hour meeting only yesterday with our practice nurses and health visitors, and from this it emerged that if we are to find the time to meet certain of these screening-of-patients targets, our Well Person Clinic which we have run for the last six years will have to be curtailed, and with it some of the goodwill and understanding that these clinics generate will evaporate. Is this really what the government wants to achieve?

All these aspects of the practice were being developed and extended well before the conception of the contract or White Paper. General practice was naturally evolving all over the country in much the same way, as the result of several factors. The rapidly improved training of young qualified doctors specific- ally for general practice was a tremendous advance, and con- tinuing postgraduate education for established practitioners was fast developing. General practice was getting proper recognition as a department of medicine in its own right and enthusiasm was in the air. Compare this with the terrible clinical isolation I remember so well when I started in practice.

At that time I was not even expected to talk to the 'other practice' at the end of the High Street, and to talk clinical matters with other doctors in other places seemed somehow impossible. At this time general practice seemed to me to be in a solitary, miserable and unrespected nose-dive into obscurity. However I then began to attend some of the medical meetings held at such places as Leeds Infirmary. These were strictly didactic in style, and held, it always seemed, on Sunday afternoons.

It was only over tea at such meetings that I discovered I could actually talk to other general practitioners, and we began to generate our own ideas about postgraduate education. I began to realise that you didn't have to work in Harley Street or indeed be a consultant to have succeeded. I felt an enthusiasm amounting to excitement about having a hand in designing the future of general practice. Certain that our ideas would prosper, we realised that we could become specialists in the most important field: people.

I suddenly recognised the most obvious, and yet the most dynamic truth. It is general practice that provides that vital first contact with the patient. Patients do not often come with disease, but with problems, from which diagnoses can sometimes be determined. In the more recently developed field of preventive medicine, the GP reaches out to patients, either for a consultation in the surgery or at home or via various health promotional clinics. GPs need help with this vital task, and the Primary Care Team of nurses, health visitors and other health promoters have been closely involved in its development. Historically, however, many general practitioners were slow to help facilitate this development, and it was probably into this gap that the medical bureaucrats began to pour and develop in their trifid chrysalises. This is not to say that medical administrative assistance is not necessary; indeed, one might ask whether a 12–15 billion pound a year organisation like the Health Service should be run on 30 per cent of the organisational staff that a multinational company of the same turnover would have.

However, national health care and promotion is not a multinational business aimed at profit. At most, it could be said to be aimed at individuals so that they remain healthy in order to make a profit for themselves.

Over the past twenty years general practice has been undergoing a natural and accelerating evolution into what I believe is the best primary health care service in the world. The general practitioner contract of April 1990 and the White Paper will both have been compelled upon general practitioners and the country. They threaten to throttle this natural and healthy evolution and provide a haven for the legions of medical bureaucrats, a nightmare for the Primary Care Team and nigh on an administrative impossibility for the new Family Health Service Authorities, as the Family Practitioner Committees have now been renamed. The leaders of these committees are newly appointed on political grounds, and government have thereby removed professional, democratic and consumer influences almost entirely from this administration.

DURING AUGUST 1989 we had four early morning meetings to consider the implications of the contract and White Paper. As a result, we determined to try and do something about it. On 4 September we entertained Geoffrey Rivett from the Department of Health and Social Security who had dinner and stayed the night at my house with his wife, Barbara. We had prepared carefully and constructively for this meeting, at which all partners were present. I started with some general questions and each partner had a particular area upon which to concentrate. I began by commenting to our guest that the contract and White Paper were being forced upon a system of health care which had been evolved and weathered by time and practice. Would Dr Rivett agree that most of the contract and Paper was based on totally untried hypotheses, largely thought out by people who were in ivory towers miles from the front line of general practice? We were staggered when after a few moments thought he said, 'Yes, I largely agree!'

I can only say that the more the discussion went on, the more we realised what a nightmare it was going to be. A mood of dejection hung over our normally vibrant practice for the next few days. General practice was being throttled and hung there with its legs kicking. I wondered if it was too late to revive it.

The care of our patients and our relationships with some of them are simply not going to be as good as they were. The changes to the Health Service can only dissolve and evaporate away any vestige of goodwill on our part. I am quite sure that the government has grossly undervalued the importance of this goodwill which is an essential lubricant in running the machinery of primary medical care in this country.

I WALKED UP to the surgery early today in order to attack some more of the paperwork. Tom, our cleaner, was already in the waiting room polishing a brass plaque which commemorated a certain proud day back in 1982.

It was on 14 July of that year that my partners, our architect and all of our wives attended a ceremony at the Ritz Hotel, London. The practice had won a competition for the best functional surgery building in the United Kingdom, and Kenneth Clarke, the Minister for Health, was to make his presentation.

As he presented me with the brass plaque, Mr Clarke said, 'Very well done, I only wish there were more practices like yours in the country.'

I now regarded that same plaque gleaming on our waiting room wall after Tom's efforts. I wondered what Kenneth Clarke would say to me today, or for that matter what I'd like to say to him.

SOMETIMES, DRIVING HOME FROM an evening call or meeting at the hospital, I will look for a light on the outside corner of Skirbeck farmhouse. Tonight I spied the light, and knew that Robin was in and mixing.

As I stepped from the car the five sheep-dogs barked their greeting and I tapped a tune on the sitting-room window. Robin opened the back door with a chuckle – he'd already switched on the electric kettle. Even Henry Dugdale of Borrins Farm, himself an expert in this field, will admit that no one can mix a hot toddy like Robin.

We sat with glasses in hand, and the talk was gentle with the odd laugh as we recalled some event past and gone. Then Robin asked me if there was anything that I'd really wanted to own in the past, and never managed to win. 'Not really,' I replied, 'only my picture.'

'How do you mean "your picture"?' he asked, puzzled. So I told him, after he'd returned from the kitchen with another of his square-patterned tumblers, the markings on which seem to enable him to mix to such perfection.

Well, I began, I used to know a lovely old couple who lived in Mill Close in Settle. Irene started life as a landlady's daughter in Millom, Barrow in Furness. Julian Perski was one of a large Polish family who ran a bakery in the town of Krakow. His father had been killed and as a result Julian had been forced to take up baking at the tender age of seven to help support the family. Eventually he became an excellent and respected pastry cook in his home town.

War intervened and Julian joined the army, where he found himself with General Anders fighting his way from Egypt right through to the storming of Monte Cassino. Later he arrived in England, took rooms in Millom and after some time married the landlady's daughter, Irene.

Irene and Julian came to Settle in the Sixties when Julian started baking for Helmut Francmanis, the Polish baker in the market square. After what must have been a comparatively uneventful but happy few years he retired, with no children and no relatives.

They both suffered little bits of this and that, and over the years I saw quite a lot of them. Because they were on their own

I used to sit and talk to them, and occasionally Julian would bring out some strong Polish spirit in a peculiar tall bottle. We would drink it under the smiling eyes of an old man who gazed out at us from a lovely oil painting which hung on their wall. This wrinkled but happy figure had been captured sitting in a farm kitchen playing a concertina to the delight of a young lady and her mother, whose faces glowed with pleasure. It encapsulated what I imagined to be a typical Dutch scene of country life in the past.

Irene must have noticed my eyes being drawn to it because on several occasions she said that I would receive the picture when they were gone, a remark which doctors hear occasionally and shrug off with a laugh. I didn't like to inspect the picture closely; I only knew it was a joyful scene and I liked it.

Julian died and Irene moved to a bungalow in Hellifield where she hung the picture on the sitting-room wall. 'When I go that's yours,' she would say to me regularly during my weekly call on this now lonely widow.

She died peacefully one February day, leaving behind her few belongings. It was well known in the village that she wanted a certain lamp to be given to Mrs so and so, and a table to another friend, and of course the painting was to be given to the doc, so the warden on the estate advised me to go and pick it up. However Irene died intestate, so bureaucracy became involved. A valuer came in for the Crown, and surprisingly quickly everything, including my painting, disappeared to Harrogate. I only knew that the picture 'belonged' to me and I wanted it for its beauty and because it had been given to me by this somewhat eccentric dear old lady. A solicitor told me to write to the Bona Vacantia division of the treasury department, which I did, receiving a rather unhelpful note in return saying that unless I had further evidence of a claim I would have to bid at the auction. I was tempted to ask some of Irene's friends and neighbours who all knew the story to witness my claim, but you have to be wary in the area of gifts since it wouldn't do to even seed the thought that the doc is out to gain from a patient's death in any way. Then I discovered the valuer expected bids to start at £5000.

I had never thought how much it might be worth, but felt that as soon as it turned out to be valuable, my ability to try any harder to win it back might be misconstrued. I went across to Harrogate to have a last look at the picture on the viewing day before the sale. It was on the floor, propped up against the wall, half-hidden under a big sideboard. I thought this was odd as it must have been the star piece of the sale, and indeed was featured as such in a colour photograph as the title page of the catalogue. I also phoned the auctioneers a few days before and asked the lady if I might have a copy of this photograph of the picture. 'Certainly,' she had replied, and suggested a reasonable size, so that I could have it framed. I later received another phone call from this embarrassed lady to say I couldn't possibly have a copy photograph, and she rang off. It may have had something to do with copyright, but I was bemused by the way in which it seemed to me the auctioneers were almost trying to bury the painting so it might be forgotten.

I had to be away in London on the day of the sale and never discovered what it sold for, or where it went. But one thing's for sure: I know it will always be my picture in the eyes of Irene and myself, and I'm sure Julian would have given his thumbs up to it as well.

I SIPPED the last of Robin's hot toddy and got up to go. 'So that's the only thing I ever really wanted but lost from the past,' I said to Robin with a wry smile, 'my painting by Van Rampigi.'

EVENING SURGERY on the second Monday of every month is always a little fraught because by 7 p.m. I have to be 12 miles away at the meeting of the governers of Bentham School. Our daughters Sammy and Katie went to school at Bentham and over the years I've become more involved in the governing body, indeed this year I'm chairman.

On this particular Monday there were two extra dimensions to the evening, and a third, unknown to any of us, was about to be slotted in. Firstly, before the governers' meeting, I had arranged to meet the school cleaners because I wanted to listen to their views on ideas which have been proposed for their department; and secondly the television camera crew were to accompany me in my car. The third unexpected element was a motorcyclist who had done a sort of Evel Knievel just moments before we rounded a long corner halfway to Bentham.

We were discussing the restoration work being done on the wreck of a barn, when we came upon a van and an articulated tanker pulled over onto the right-hand side of the road on the brow of the hill. It wasn't the place to stop to pass the time of day and I started to look for signs of a collision between the vehicles. As I slowed, we could see no evidence of damage, nor was either driver to be seen. I was about to drive on, assuming one or other vehicle had simply broken down, when one of the camera crew glanced to our left and noticed a short section of the dry stone wall missing, the gap revealing the crumpled shape of a motorcyle lying at the bottom of a drop of several feet. Lying in the grass beyond this was the supine figure of its rider.

I pulled in 30 yards further on, switched on my hazard warning lights, and ran back to the field. As we scrambled down the 8-foot bank towards the leather-clad motorcyclist, I asked the lorry driver to go to the rear end of the scene to warn traffic of the danger around the blind corner. The last thing we wanted was another accident.

The van driver tried to explain what had happened as I examined the motorcyclist. He thought the poor fellow had lost it on the corner, hit the back of the van and run out of road, forcing him to take flight over the 8-foot banking. The huge articulated tanker had taken fright and just managed to miss the van.

First aid at road traffic accidents is in the order of airway, breathing and circulation, then triage which is army terminology for deciding which casualties are most urgently in need of hospitalisation. In this case triage was not a problem, since it was clear that only one person was injured.

The casualty was moaning with each expiration, indicating he was alive and probably had a reasonably clear airway. His eyes were closed, but opened on my demand, and the pupils were equal, so his consciousness level seemed satisfactory at the moment. I was concerned about the mechanical effects that his acrobatic leap might have had on his spine.

His tight-fitting red leather outfit may have saved him from a good deal of superficial injury, but it also made it difficult to examine the contents. I was sure he had a broken right arm, and was assuming he had a spinal injury until this was proved otherwise. My assumption was based on the factors of force, distance and trajectory from the high bank and the condition of the crumpled motorbike.

The crash helmet was more difficult to remove than I imagined, as I tried to be careful of his cervical spine. But already things were looking better for Nigel. The fact that he'd given me his name told me that much. Also he had moved all four limbs actively; he was regaining colour and consciousness rather than losing them; and we had a bevy of helpers when the time came to lift Nigel on to the stretcher when the ambulance arrived. This would be soon because the driver of the artic had used his cab radio to summon help.

Once I knew all the major parameters were satisfactory, I could look at Nigel's thumb which I had noticed was dislocated. As I did so he was better enough to tell me to leave it alone. I reassured him I was a doctor, which he questioned – understandably considering my instant appearance on the scene. I distracted his attention and his thumb simultaneously and thereby reduced the dislocation. One of his problems solved at least.

It's always interesting to read one of the many books available on the subject of first aid and road traffic accident management – by the fireside where it all appears easy. It's another story in the field where the combination of noise, commotion, over-the-top reaction, wet, dirt, groans and brave silent suffering can make things altogether different and more difficult.

The ambulance arrived and I was glad of the team of hands because we were able to lift Nigel on to the stretcher keeping him and his spine straight. Then with the help of the whole camera crew, the ambulance men and the two lorry drivers, the stretcher was gently but confidently lifted up to road level, keeping it horizontal, despite the height of the bank.

As we drove our separate ways, I noticed the thistles in the field looked as though nothing had ever happened.

My only problem was how to convince the Bentham school cleaners that my unconscionable lateness was due to a genuinely unexpected attendance at a road accident.

I STEELED MYSELF to carry out a killing this morning. Scottie has been insistent that I had to dispatch the youngster whose early morning vocal exercises have become a real nuisance lately. It's not a job I enjoy doing, but when it has to be performed there's no time for sentimentality.

It seemed a pity to dispose of the young one since he's the best breeder, but he's definitely the noisier of the two. I loaded a cartridge into the barrel of my 4:10 shotgun, put on the ear defenders and walked out into the back garden as stealthily as possible. I needed to perform the deed where the high stone wall made accidents from ricochets unlikely, and observation by passing patients impossible. I'm not sure the sight of the doc shooting down a helpless victim would be the best way of encouraging confidence in either my attitudes or my abilities.

As I moved through the hedge which leads to the garden I saw my target. The safety catch slipped off with a flick of my thumb and I raised the gun to my shoulder. He saw me and began to race across the lawn – at least he wasn't standing still. I swung slowly through and fired. Fred II, as he had been nicknamed, gave a squawk of protest, a last flap of his wings and our rather fine cockerel departed this world.

I felt like Macbeth after Duncan's murder, and transferred some of the blame, and the guilt I felt, onto Scottie, who had urged me on to such a foul deed.

We'd not actually received complaints from the neighbours but, despite their kindness and tolerance, I'm sure complaints were imminent. Fred II's internal alarm clock seemed to be on a different time zone from the rest of Settle and his regular cock-a-doodle-do reveille at 03.30 hours was becoming a little embarrassing. In a remote farmyard it might have been acceptable, even expected. In the middle of a market town it was less impressive.

I think Scottie was upset when the cull had finally been completed, having raised the chap from an egg. We're now back down to one, older, cockerel, which is better for everyone concerned, including the hens. They make a token show of lifting their wings in response to his mating displays, but he doesn't really bother them much these days.

We've kept 'practice hens' on our paddock at the side of the house for some fifteen years. The doctor on duty shuts them up each night and collects the eggs laid that day. Because we're so nearby, Scottie sees to them in the mornings. In this way the families have been involved in their care, particularly when chicks have hatched, and this is the smallest illustration of our practice philosophy. All five partners live close by, three of us within 100 yards of the surgery. Indeed it's part of the practice agreement that we live within a mile of the surgery. This not only promotes neighbourly family relationships but makes it possible to arrange meetings easily.

We find a useful time for meetings is 7.30 in the morning, when it's unusual for the duty doctor to be called and our minds are alert. The subject discussed at many of our gatherings lately has inevitably been the White Paper, but we also spend time on more worthwhile and purposeful subjects such as pharmacy drug stocks, practice policies, or the planning of a research project. Don't let me give the impression that we like getting up early, but such meetings are made necessary in today's medico-political climate. We do also manage to have more sociable evening gatherings with glass in hand.

It is vital to maintain the infrastructure of a general practice. There are certain times and meetings to which a high priority must be given. Our 8.30 to 9.00 a.m. phone-in begins our day, and each morning during this half hour our health visitors and district nurses come into the surgery to liaise with us. On Tuesdays there is a full meeting of the Primary Care Team. This will vary in number from fifteen to twenty, with physiotherapy, home help service, social services, the old people's residential home, Age Concern, occupational therapy, community mental health and educational psychology all being represented. The core team of doctors, nurses and health visitors join in this meeting, which is held in the surgery common room after the phone-in. It gives everyone the opportunity to discuss a particular patient's needs on a one-to-one basis or with a larger group of relevant carers.

At 1.00 p.m. on Fridays the doctors and practice manager meet at the home of the weekend duty doctor for our practice lunch. It's our chance to discuss important matters, and is where practice problems can be discussed frankly on a regular basis. The fact that it's held at each of our homes in turn exercises that little bit of bonding which is an essential flavour of a cohesive country practice.

FRIDAY

25

MAY

I'VE SPENT A GOOD DEAL of time today while I've been driving on my rounds, reflecting on a meeting at the surgery this morning. It was the latest attempt to find a solution to a case which has been worrying me for a long time.

It concerns a widow and her son. The mother, Isabella, is getting on in years, and at eighty-three her health is beginning to fail. In normal circumstances we would care for her with the help of our primary care team of nurses, health visitors and others, but in her case there's an added complication. Her son, Michael, is both physically and mentally handicapped and requires much attention.

When Michael was forty-two he suffered a bleed into the tissues surrounding the brain, which has left him with a crippling mental impairment; then six years later he had a coronary thrombosis which took its toll physically. Now at fifty-two years old he is quite unable to live on his own.

Isabella is a remarkably brave woman who is quite determined to look after her son; and this she does with well-intentioned love and tolerance. Unfortunately the care and attention she has lavished upon him has rendered him even more dependent.

Our task this morning was to gaze into a crystal ball, hoping to reveal the future for Michael in the light of the inevitable prospect that his mother may die at any time. Hunched around the tea leaves were our own primary care team with additional social services people. My biggest fear at the moment is that if Isabella were to die, Michael might do something silly or irrational in response. In the past he has talked of committing suicide when she goes, and the very fact that he's expressed such thoughts is obviously worrying, even if we think it unlikely he would actually carry them through.

Another aspect of Isabella's understandable over-protection of him is that she insists he's not able to do anything for or by himself. She says that he can't even climb the stairs on his own. His heart complaint obviously does have some bearing on this, but I suspect this inability is mainly due to her reinforcement of the idea that he can't do it. What is clear from all the assessments

Overleaf: Ken at Sowerthwaite Farm

which have been made of him is that he really won't be able to manage on his own at home.

As a result of the meeting we decided that our short-term plan would be to transfer him into one of our local private nursing homes where they have the staff to observe and look after him, until a more permanent solution is found. The only other option seemed to be the psychiatric wards at Airedale Hospital – and in Michael's case we decided this option was inappropriate, and certainly not what his mother would want.

On the other hand Isabella is fairly indestructible and our preparations may well be premature. I have tried looking into crystal balls before, and I can't say I'd make a fortune as a teller, in the gypsy or medical fields. Not too long ago Isabella was ill, and during that time we were able to persuade her to accept some outside assistance. She found this so helpful that she allowed it to continue after she'd recovered.

It is only by seizing upon such chance happenings that these sorts of cases can be manipulated for the better. Hence the importance of continued vigilance in circumstances which would appear to be rolling on inexorably, and therefore might be left alone to do so. Once again it's all about maintaining communication between those involved. This requires time, and now and again lately I feel time gnawing at my very soul.

DR BREWSTER has been transformed into Major Brewster for the weekend. I'm on one of my irregular Territorial Army weekends with 201 General Hospital, Royal Army Medical Corps. I've been involved with various branches of the TA since I was roped in to 12/13 Para by Larry L'Estrange.

It's been a pretty frustrating sort of day so far. There's been a lot of sitting and standing around waiting, which is why I decided to disappear and spend some time sitting on my small iron bunk on top of a coarse, hairy blanket, writing this entry in the diary, before the next group of casualties arrive.

We're simulating a general hospital, three stages removed from the front line of battle. I'm in charge of the section which receives casualties who have already been given immediate first aid at the Regimental Aid Post, and our principal task is to assess their immediate needs and give them priorities so that they can either be moved to pre-op prior to surgery in theatre, or, in less severe cases, can be dressed and sent to the wards. I think the war must be going pretty well for us so far, since we haven't seen many casualties. It's been like periods during real action – more waiting than operating. But waiting is what happens in war.

The only diversion so far was a black state Nuclear, Biological or Chemical (NBC) alert. This involves struggling into indescribably uncomfortable stiff grey-green fibresuits known unaffectionately as 'Noddy' suits; then finally donning a gas mask which looks far more sinister than I remember gas masks looking in the wartime days of my childhood. In NBC conditions our surgeons work in an operating theatre set up in a large tent, with airlocks controlling the entrance and exit. Because the air is filtered, surgeons can work in the tent without the 'Noddy' suits, in supposedly clean conditions.

The NBC alert must be one of the soldiers' most unpopular exercises, since it inevitably involves everyone becoming hot and testy. To make up for the discomfort, I've been thinking back shamelessly to my first meeting with the services at a time when 'Noddy' suits hadn't been thought of, and the most uncomfortable dress was the kilt and sporran.

I WAS INVITED to present myself for National Service at Fort George near Inverness just two weeks after the end of school term.

I was just eighteen and not really too upset about this turn of events. Although I was interested in the area of medicine and biology, I wasn't sure precisely what I wanted to do for a career, and anyway the idea of army life held some appeal for me. The next thing I knew I was in the back of a three-tonner taking me from Inverness to Fort George.

We drove along the peninsula sticking out into the Moray Firth and caught our first glimpse of the grim pile which was to be home for the next sixteen weeks. As we approached the fort in the cold, grey afternoon light and the portcullis was raised, I began to wonder if I'd got it right. I felt an immediate empathy with the French Napoleonic prisoners of war who were sent into isolation and exile on the island of St Helena, and who until just a few weeks before had been meaningless historical figures in my school cert examination papers.

I had been led to believe that public school was tough but character-building. I soon realised I knew and had experienced nothing. It had in fact been relatively soft and very cloistered. This was the real world.

Of the five other conscripts in my stone-faced barrack room two were brickies from the Gorbals area of Glasgow, another was a window-cleaner who delighted in detailing the 'things he had seen from his ladder', also from the Queen of cities. The fourth was a professional safebreaker, the rest of whose history I never discovered, and the last, 'Boy Mac', was even more of an enigma. I tried to ask him something about his background once. I didn't try twice.

Ten days before, metaphorically at least, I'd been in short trousers, now I was in élite company.

I remember, for example, my first experience of breakfast: kippers served on chipped enamel plates. I made the mistake of picking up my knife and fork and became aware of others looking at me as they tucked in using just their hands. The kippers were so well done it was like eating biscuits. That innocent example of etiquette gave away my distinctly different background.

Throughout the early days I was aware that my English accent, albeit with its Yorkshire twang, marked me out from the others, but never so vividly as on our first night off.

Eight weeks into our training we were allowed into Inverness in the back of three-ton trucks, knowing that if we didn't get back by eleven o'clock we would be in big trouble.

We inevitably fell into the nearest pub. Being a Friday night, all the drinkers there were already somewhat under the influence.

Having downed a pint or two we really had begun to enjoy our brief newfound freedom when suddenly I became aware of the locals around the bar looking at me. To say they started to take exception to my English accent and ancestry is perhaps the politest way I can describe their taunts. I was moments away from having my visual identity drastically changed when my five companions moved around me like a phalanx. Up to this point I'd been the object of their jibes about my Englishness; suddenly the suggestion that anyone else should malign my accent or lay a finger on me turned them into stalwart defenders, and me into one of their own. If any one of the locals had touched me they would have suffered grievous bodily harm courtesy of the legion surrounding me. For a moment it was like a tense bar-room scene from a Wild West movie, but drinks on the house from a quick-witted and prudent landlord broke the spell before any fists flew.

It was my first experience of the way real group loyalty can quash social and ethnic differences – a revelation I will never forget.

THE DRILL SERGEANTS were tough men. In those days there was a uniformity in the way they ran affairs: they all bawled everyone out for everything, some more viciously than others. In the middle of the sixteen weeks' training some bright spark took it into his head to pick me out as a PO, potential officer. This meant I had to go to Catterick to attend the War Office Selection Board, which in due course passed me.

This was like a red rag to the drill sergeants. Some of them saw it as their last chance to get at these potential officers before they escaped their clutches. I vividly remember one drill sergeant ordering a soldier to fetch a fire bucket full of cold water and a scrubbing brush to scrub the face of a PO who he felt had not shaved correctly that morning.

I was comparatively lucky in that I was a bit of an athlete at the time and, as a member of the recruits' team, I was allowed to run out on the Moray sands as part of my training while everyone else was confined to the fort. I would run for many miles along the sands, away from the shore into the mists, suddenly encountering great flocks of geese. I treasured these opportunities to run and think and be away from soldiers for a few hours, with only these majestic birds for company.

It was during this period that I damaged my hearing in one ear as we were training to use 2-inch mortars. Number 2 mortar man would drop the small, finned shells down a short drainpipe-like tube, one end of which was dug into the ground. After he had knelt back in position, and not before, number 2 would command number 1 mortar man to fire. I was number 2 and my number 1 was a Hebridean Island boy who was not used to waiting for orders – a fact I was not to realise until he had pulled the trigger before I could remove myself, and my ears, from the blast line. My left ear was treated to the full lateral blast from the barrel.

The ear hummed a bit, but I kept a stiff upper lip and said nowt. I'm sure if I had said some'at, I would now be the beneficiary of a small army pension.

The worst problem I'm left with is that I can't pick out one person's speech in crowded, noisy situations. Cocktail party chat I'm quite happy to miss, but over a pint of my favourite beer, Tetleys, at *The Old Station* I sometimes miss some of the repartee, and must be considered a dull boy on occasions.

At the end of sixteen weeks of this 'basic training' we were to have a passing-out parade. Having seen many similar parades on the fort's square, led by the pipe and drums of the Seaforth Highlanders, I looked forward to this as the event which would make all the hard times worthwhile, but it was not to be. Just before the parade I was whisked away to the Officer Cadet Training Unit at Eaton Hall, Chester, and was therefore deprived of the opportunity to take my rightful place in the proceedings. I shall always remember feeling hurt and cheated by this exclusion. By then the ragged phalanx which had protected me in the pub had become a tough group bound together by mutual respect. I thought it a dreadful example of man management by my commanders not to realise the importance to me of taking my place alongside them in the final parade. I wonder if any of 'my five' felt the same. I hope they did.

EATON HALL, previously the home of the Duke of Westminster, was all spit and polish. It was a first-class experience where we learnt quickly to work together as a team. In physical exercises the men who were best at strength and distance would carry the gear for the others who couldn't manage it. That way we all finished together in good time for the sake of the group. On other occasions those better at tactics looked after planning and helped through the less academic amongst us. It was a great lesson in mutual mental and physical trust.

In February 1949 we marched in our passing-out parade and received our commissions. We were then dispersed and posted to our various regiments. I was sent to join the 1st Battalion Argyll and Sutherland Highlanders at Colchester.

The station was a real brassbuttons and bullshit place. It was an extremely expensive mess and all my pay went straight into settling the weekly mess bill. This was still in the days when many of the other officers had private incomes and weren't so sharply affected by economic considerations.

I was of a different social background to the rest of the officers and definitely less worldly wise. One officer who did his best to ease me into the way of life told me months later about an occasion when, unwittingly, I caused much amusement in the refined atmosphere of the mess. I was standing by the open fire lifting my kilt up to warm my bum when he came in and asked me how I was doing. I apparently replied, 'Ee, reet good, but brass is tight.'

I'm sure he exaggerated my Yorkshire accent, but it pointed up the problem I might have encountered of not fitting in with the gentlemen officers. I couldn't help thinking back a few months to 'my five' comrades at Fort George and how then I'd been painfully aware of what seemed like a public school accent in comparison with their tough Glasgow Gorbals speech, and I felt even more deeply my regret and anger at missing that final parade.

During my time in Colchester I had a choice to make. I could request a Class B release in order to take up my studies at university the following October, in which case I would continue to soldier at home. The alternative was to stay on with the regiment and hope for a foreign posting.

I decided on the latter and two months later embarked on the ship the *Empire Trouper* berthed at Southampton and bound for Hong Kong.

OUR FIRST BILLETS in Hong Kong were splendid, especially for those days. They were on the south end of the island at Stanley, overlooking the sea. The officers' mess was a magnificent sight, yards of long white balconies overlooking the South China Sea. For a young green second lieutenant, sitting sipping gin at sunset watching the odd junk sailing through the reflection of the setting sun, this was quite something.

After three months of this tough life, we were despatched to camp in the New Territories at Tan Mai. Here we found ourselves on full alert, apparently awaiting an invasion by the 'Commies' who were poised just across the border.

The training was intense, with exciting full-brigade exercises. We lived under canvas, survived typhoons in conditions far from the luxury of Stanley, but all the more enjoyable for that. I began to realise that I appreciated the discipline. It gave me an order of life and a respect for people who apparently knew less in purely educational terms but who were very capable in their own fields and knew so much more of the world than me.

I shared a tent with four other chaps and a brightly coloured noisy fifth co-tenant we'd acquired in Hong Kong's famous Bird Street market. Murdo the cockatoo lived mainly outside the tent, tethered to the guy ropes by his leg. He was a brilliant impersonator who had unfortunately chosen to specialise in sound effects rather than voices. His favourite, judging by the frequency of its performance, was the sound of spitting, which he'd mastered to an unnervingly accurate degree. It became his dawn chorus, and we'd be woken at four in the morning by the loudest hawking you can imagine. If we were really lucky this would be followed by a long burst of early morning smoker's cough at penetrating volume.

He also looked forward to our ablutions, which bore more resemblance to a bird bath than anything else. There was little water, so a 'shower' consisted of standing in a bowl and using a jug to recycle the water over your head. Murdo would bide his time and wait until you were completely naked and standing in the bowl covered in soap, whereupon he would attack the back of your knees, pausing only to cackle.

The New Territories were served by a road system roughly in the shape of an inverted pyramid. A road led up one coastal side of the triangle from Kowloon to one end of the Chinese border, then along the border to the far end, forming the base of the triangle. From there another road made its way south to Kowloon along the other coast. Clinging to the side of the hills and cliffs, these roads proved too much for army trucks and drivers on a number of occasions. There were several accidents when vehicles had suddenly confronted each other and one or both had been knocked off the track to fall down the cliffs, often with fatal results. The top brass decided to introduce a one-way system around the triangle in an attempt to avoid further accidents. I remember it was anti-clockwise because it went down past the San Miguel factory.

Unfortunately this didn't prevent several further accidents. At one point our commanders became so annoyed at the continued fatalities that they decreed there should be no wheeled vehicles on the roads over the following weekend.

A mood of gloom descended on the Friday evening mess gathering as we all realised our weekend of fun had been curtailed. Some of the lads muttered about the beautiful girls waiting for them in town, others dreamt of the ice-cold Tiger beers being poured at that very moment in expectation of their arrival. With the only other prospect being to walk the 40 miles we felt sure we had been well and truly gated.

Then one of the officers, Dougie Ross, who had been sitting quietly and staring into his warm beer, let out a sound which could almost have been 'Eureka'. Ignoring our questions, he disappeared.

He was in charge of S company, the support blokes. About fifteen minutes later there was a great rumbling sound outside the mess and when we ran out there was Dougie at the controls of a Bren Gun carrier. We were open-mouthed. 'You can't do that,' we gasped, in various states of disbelief, as we realised the shape of his plan. 'I can,' he said. 'The order states no *wheeled* vehicles to be driven on the roads.' The carrier before us sat on caterpillar tracks.

We didn't think too long about how many rules we were breaching, but simply jumped aboard and roared off towards the promised delights awaiting us in town.

Dougie negotiated the treacherous road, and then drove along Nathan Road, the main road, right into the Peninsula Hotel between the Bentleys and Rolls-Royces. As we disembarked from our unorthodox taxi, in front of one of the top hotels in the world, Dougie jumped down from the vehicle, strolled across to one of the doormen who had just finished parking a Rolls-Royce, and nonchalantly gave him the keys, saying, 'Try parking that bloody thing!'

I SPENT OVER a year in Hong Kong before my demob number came up. I returned to Britain on a boat which seemed determined to destroy its passengers by making us seasick to the point where no one could really care whether we got back home or not. All that changed as we entered home waters and we arrived in Southampton demob happy. I had forgotten how green England was.

MUCH OF THE day-to-day care Willie Morphet receives is from several neighbours, but particularly from Freda and John Booth who live across the grass forecourt of this ancient farmstead. Only people who understand Willie's erratic ways would tolerate him anyway. Today on the phone Freda was telling me that 'someone' has driven over the outmeadow and run down a length of the electric fence along with two of the supporting stanchions. Perhaps this might at least put Willie off buying his new car for a while.

Talking to John the other day I was reminded of what an incredible recovery he himself had made from his accident which happened in early December in the cold winter of 1980. That morning John had been fixing up drive power for a pump by way of a rotating shaft from the tractor, so that he could transfer slurry from the glamorously named lagoon into the tank of the spreader. John had returned to the job after lunch, in the cold afternoon, smothered in pullovers and coats. He bent over the rotating power take-off, which seized his coat sleeve and in one movement hurled him round and over the top of the revolving shaft, smashing his body down on the floor at the other side. Such was the force of this impact that mercifully it stalled the engine, but not before John had suffered terrible compound and multiple fractures of his right leg, and broken every rib on the left side of his chest. By chance his brother Eric came around to see how John was doing and discovered the accident.

At Airedale hospital the injuries were treated, but after some twenty-four hours John's consciousness level began to fluctuate, so he was taken to Leeds neurosurgery unit. There his condition worsened and he was put on a ventilator, on which he remained for three anxious days.

The cause of John's cerebral problem was fat embolism. Tiny globules of fat from the fracture site became lodged in the blood vessels of the brain, interfering with the blood supply to part of the brain.

Anxious days were not yet over for Freda, who was doing a round trip of 100 miles daily to visit John. Even with the cerebral problem identified, and after he'd come off the ventilator, there was still no response from him. She remembered, 'He just lay there breathing and that's all he'd do. Eyes open, not blinking,

'Willie, you're not to drive!'
'I can't promise . . .'

no smile, no expression, nothing for eight days.' Then he'd twitched, and the long and slow process of nursing him back to health began.

Power take-offs should be much respected and never regarded as safe, no matter how many guards are placed around them. Indeed any powered rotating agricultural shaft can cause problems and as Brian Lambert laconically put it to me the other day, 'These bits of machines don't really seem to care, and they don't take notice of you either.'

Brian came in today for a routine check-up which included the injured hand he has been carrying for some years now.

It was hay time and the wagon-loads of baled hay were coming in well. Brian was standing on top of a stack, or 'hay moo', and receiving the bales from the upper end of a mechanical elevator, then stacking them within the barn. One bale went up the lift with the ends of a piece of baler twine hanging loose underneath. As Brian put both hands under the bale to get hold of it, one end of the loose piece of twine twisted around his thumb where it became firmly wrapped. At the same moment the other end caught around the rotating mechanical shaft which powered the moving belt and drew him closer to the shaft with every turn. It was set to pull his thumb, hand and arm towards and right around, the shaft, like fishing line on a reel. With all the noise of the elevator and engine the chap below, Billy Foster, was completely oblivious of what was going on, and was therefore no help. Brian realised what was in danger of happening and on the spur of the moment pulled away with all his might in an attempt to break the twine. He is a big strapping chap and thought at first that he'd been successful, and had probably just broken his thumb. However, when he looked down he realised he'd done slightly more damage. Where his thumb had been there was now a cavity. He'd totally avulsed his thumb: pulled it right off.

It was only when he managed to climb down from the hay moo that Billy realised that anything was wrong. They bound the wound with the only piece of cloth they could find and we rushed Brian to hospital where they tidied him up.

When they returned to work the thumb was found bound to the shaft by the baler twine at the top of the elevator. It stuck there like a rather macabre battle trophy for nearly three weeks before anyone had the courage to retrieve it.

Talking to Brian today, he says it's no problem as far as he's concerned in his life and work. However, he is less a thumb, which really is quite an important digit in evolutionary terms because it facilitates the movement of opposition by which we can grip things with dexterity, and is part of the reason we are where we are and not still hanging in the trees.

Farms are full of traps for the unwary and even the most careful. At just this time of year three years ago George Parkinson was working like a beaver trying to finish off silo time. The other workers had just gone into Holme farmhouse for tea. George said he would just fettle the engine of one of the tractors which was standing there with its shovel of big bale silo tines lifted up on the hydraulic rams. Silo tines are 56 inches long, as thin as your little finger, slightly curved, and extremely sharp. As George walked away from the front of the tractor and beneath the shovel it dropped like some enormous guillotine. One of the shining steel tines pierced the upper rear part of George's left calf and, being curved convexly, made a clean exit wound from the lower end of the calf, pinning George to the ground very precisely. He was literally transfixed: he couldn't get anywhere near the controls; he couldn't move in any direction; he could only stand and wait whilst the others enjoyed their tea in the kitchen 50 yards away around the front of the farmhouse. They could neither see George nor hear his shouts for help.

As George's mug of tea grew cold, someone went out to see where the heck he was, 'and he wasn't moving far, wasn't our George!' one of the lads recalled that night in the pub.

The shovel was hydraulically and most gingerly lifted, and the tine withdrawn before a spellbound audience. I examined the injured leg and cleaned the wound as best I could, then stitched both entry and exit wounds, injecting antibiotics and anti-tetanus vaccine, and the extraordinary thing was that it healed without any infection. George never looked back.

Certainly it was a good thing he hadn't looked back at the tractor at the time of his transfixion, or else it might have been his skull that the tine penetrated and not his calf.

To MY GREAT DELIGHT the truck from the local garage pulled up this afternoon, bearing a long-awaited addition to the surgery. I've managed to procure an old operating table for our new casualty room in the surgery extension. It was sitting battered and neglected in the corner of an Aladdin's cave of a storeroom at Airedale Hospital.

It needed a quick coat of paint to tart it up, and Geoff Knights had agreed to respray it at his garage in Settle. As a result we are now the proud owners of possibly the only operating table painted in racing metallic grey.

After much advice from me about bending the knees, and being careful not to damage their backs, the lads lifted the table on to the road. It fairly sparkled in the sun as it made its journey into the surgery.

For years we've struggled with a table which was liable to tip up if a patient put his or her weight on the wrong end, and had no height adjustment mechanism. This meant we had to bend awkwardly when doing minor surgery, which is not the best position for working.

The new table can be pumped up to chest height, and tilted to suit. It's also on casters so it can be moved around to make the best use of space. I hope this will help my bad back!

I could have done with it earlier today when we had an old boy to stitch up after a fall he'd had in the square. He was in quite a state, having grazed his hands and ripped the skin up quite badly. It's amazing what damage gravel can do when old people fall. They fall heavily because they lack agile protective reflexes, and the tissues are weaker and less viable.

Later in the morning I found myself bending again, this time over a tennis elbow. Its owner, Pam, works at Castleberg Hospital and has been suffering from the complaint without having been near a tennis court. She thinks it happened when she banged it, but having had a look at it I'm pretty sure it is caused by repeated rotation of the forearm under stress – the sort of action you do when you're screwing in lots of tight screws or cutting a hedge with a pair of blunt shears.

All the muscles of supination rotate the forearm in one direction and are inserted into the elbow at one point, which is where the force is concentrated when a rotating action is used. The bony

Ward duty at Castleberg Hospital

point of attachment is called the epicondyle and it is this point which becomes inflamed and very tender to pressure. Forced straightening or extension of the bent wrist against pressure will give the same excruciating pain, known so well to sufferers of tennis elbow. All the signs were there with Pam, especially the pain she suffered when I asked her to rotate my hand. It's surprising how many daily tasks involve this rotational movement, so it can be a pretty unpleasant complaint to struggle with.

There are several methods of treatment. One is to leave it alone. That's fine if it's rested, when it will probably get better on its own. Anyone involved in any sort of housework, however, will usually be performing rotating actions many times a day, causing more tension on the point.

Secondly, you can give some anti-inflammatory agents orally, which will probably help the elbow get a little better. Unfortunately they will also act on the whole body and can possibly upset the stomach.

Thirdly, and the course of action I took with Pam, you can inject the point locally with a steroid. The only disadvantage of this localised treatment is that it hurts like hell at the time! I could sympathise because I've had mine done three times by my orthopaedic friend John Cape, after some excessive bouts of windsurfing. The rapid dramatic results, however, make the temporary suffering well worthwhile.

I explained all these points to Pam as I was preparing the injection. She had had a similar problem in her left shoulder about two months ago and it had done the job in three or four days, so she was prepared to put up with the pain of the treatment.

I felt around the elbow and pinpointed the actual spot which was causing the problem. As I marked it Pam asked if she could go to work tonight. I told her I didn't think it would be a good idea, which she seemed to shrug off as being over-cautious.

As I started the injection she went very quiet. I winced inwardly for her. The steroid is held in a thick white solution, and it is injected into a fairly non-expandable tendinous origin, so pain there is sure to be.

'The shoulder didn't hurt as much as this!' she said through clenched teeth and with her eyes screwed tightly shut. 'Can I swear?' she continued. I told her to feel free, but she didn't take up the offer.

'It's what they describe as "exquisite pain",' I explained as the last drops went in.

'I don't call that exquisite,' she replied laughing, but looking at me as though I'd lost my sanity.

With the injection over, all thoughts of returning to work had obviously vanished, because she asked what she should do when she got home.

I told her to put her arm in a sling as much as possible, just to rest the muscles and take the weight of the lower arm. I explained that if you were to cut off your forearm and put it on the scales it would weigh quite a lot, so the shoulder and elbow have to work in order to carry that weight. Moreover, wearing a sling would stop her performing any rotating actions on the arm. Even when she does go back to work after twenty-four hours, it's best to keep the sling on to remind herself and everyone else that it is still sore.

ALTHOUGH I OBVIOUSLY wouldn't wish for any new casualties, I'm looking forward to operating with our new piece of hardware, in more comfort than I did this morning.

I WAS WEEKEND DUTY DOCTOR and it turned out to be fairly throng, as we would say. Whilst I've been writing up the records and prescriptions I thought I'd jot down some of the cases to illustrate and explain the use of the word throng. There were several additional phone calls for advice which I haven't even recorded.

09.00–10.30:   A busy morning surgery. We try to keep Saturdays for urgent matters that can't wait till Monday, but some patients work away from home and some few, it seems, just like to see us on Saturday.

10.50:   Just as I left to go to the usual Saturday surgery at Giggleswick School, a call came in from Pat at Greenfoot, our old people's home. Their minibus had called to collect eighty-two-year-old Lucy Wilson from her cottage behind the square to take her to the day centre, but she hadn't answered the door. Not too much cause for concern initially, since on previous occasions she has simply been inside and not heard callers because of her deafness. I nipped up to her house and tried to make her hear me, but my efforts were to no avail. The door was still locked, and I could see no sign of anyone downstairs, which probably meant that she was still in bed. The only slight worry was the pint of milk standing on the doorstep. Lucy has sometimes locked herself away for several days, so I decided to leave it for a couple of hours and then try again. Last time this happened we got the police and they broke in only to find Lucy asleep.

11.55:   I left a shorter than usual Giggleswick School surgery, and on my way back to the car had a brief word about one of the pupils with Warwick Brookes, the Second Master.

12 noon: I called to see six-year-old Paul Atkinson at his home on the Riversdale estate in Giggleswick. He was terribly upset, having vomited several times, and apparently had stomach pains. He was crying, screaming and incredibly resistant to any examination. Eventually I managed to look at his ears and down his throat, but he wouldn't let me examine the offending stomach about which he'd been complaining 'all night'. I did manage to

have a cursory feel whilst his mother held him but all I could feel was a very rigid abdomen. So I had to assume an acute condition, possibly an unusually young appendicitis, and was thinking in terms of hospital admission. Then after I'd sat and talked on to his mother for a while, diverting his attention, he stopped crying. When he'd calmed down further and we'd built up a little bit of a relationship between us I was able to put a hand on his belly. His abdomen had become perfectly soft and I could dismiss any acute conditions, at least for the moment. I left some dicyclomine for him, to relieve the spasm in his gut. I don't really know what caused him to get so upset, but I suspect it might have been some sort of gut colic combined with a little behavioural problem. It struck me that he might have been mad with his sister who he could see running around happily, while he was in pain. I'm sure that often it is the sum of several things that gives rise to such presentations.

12.20: Back at the surgery in an effort to help our two Saturday receptionists close up not too much after their scheduled 12 noon. A wee five-year-old boy, James Dutton, came in carrying a penny – in his stomach. His parents were fairly sure he'd swallowed one and were worried. I reassured them that children pass all manner of incredible objects through the bowel, and ten to one he'll rid himself of it within a couple of days without our intervention. I sent them down to Airedale Hospital for an X-ray so we can confirm its presence and establish its present position. Then if any problem does arise we can monitor the progress of the consumed coin along the bowel with further pictures.

12.25: Audrey Hogg, Frank's wife, phoned to say he was suffering with a terribly irritating cough, which might have been associated with captopril, one of the newer drugs Frank is taking to help his heart problem. I'd already written to Paul Silverton, our cardiologist, asking him to see Frank again urgently. He has two basic and quite longstanding pathologies: achalasia, a narrowing of the oesophagus or food pipe as it nears the stomach, which means that food gets trapped at the bottom; and, secondly, a massive heart murmur.

In his case this is due to a very marked aortic stenosis, a narrowing of the main outlet from the heart, which causes the blood flow to be restricted. This generates a noise or murmur, and is rather like water squeezing through a worn tap washer. It's fairly pronounced and you can get what is known as a palpable thrill if you put your hand on his chest, when you can feel the vibrations as the blood is pushed through the narrowed valve. I told Audrey I'd be down directly.

12.45: I manoeuvred down the A65 the 5 miles to Barton House Farm. Frank was obviously distressed by the cough, and I got a feeling that the captopril is not his problem. We discussed matters and I arranged a phone review for 9.00 a.m. Sunday. I was thinking in terms of admission despite the urgent referral already made.

13.10: Two miles further on from Barton House I was visiting another Frank. Frank Beresford is 90, and had been at Harden Bridge with Willie Morphet back in March. When I asked him how he was feeling, he replied 'Champion' as usual. He is a lovely man who now has gross osteo-arthritis, a degree of heart failure, and he 'leaks a bit, you know'.

The district nurses have tried various methods of keeping him dry, including a penile sheath. Frank's long-term care is still undecided, and he is just back home from Anley, a private nursing home. Veronica, the matron there, told me of a great conversation he had with her about 'teaching me to use a condom at my age', and challenging one of the other nurses that as a married woman she ought to know how to put one on. The wretchedness of urinary incontinence is terrible, and I think I'll fit him with an indwelling catheter and spigot or bag; then he will at least be dry, and much more comfortable.

13.35: Now back in Settle and a quick look up Victoria Street to see if Lucy Wilson had emerged, or taken in the milk. She had done neither. Mrs Boardman from across the road came over and told me she hadn't seen her today, but had taken in her shopping yesterday when Lucy seemed fine. She didn't have a key but showed me around the back of the terrace of cottages, down a tiny alleyway which was strung across with washing lines at neck level. Seen in daylight it was easy to negotiate; at night you run the risk of being garrotted by the lines. We couldn't see anything through the rear windows which was neither reassuring nor unduly worrying, so, after some discussion, we decided to leave it for another couple of hours before getting the police to break in.

13.45: Scottie sat patiently in the kitchen reading the paper. A quick bowl of soup because yet another Frank had phoned just after one o'clock to say he was in some distress with a painful swelling of his penis.

14.05: Frank number three opened his door for me with a nod of 'thanks for coming', and went directly upstairs, beckoning me to follow. As I thought from the sound of the message, he had a paraphimosis, an extremely painful condition in which the foreskin becomes swollen and trapped behind the head of the penis. I have reduced these conditions before by getting the patient to use an anti-inflammatory cream for an hour or two and then manipulating the reduced swelling to its more normal position. I gave Frank the cream and told him I'd be back, but just before leaving phoned Scottie to find that a message was just in concerning Helen, who lives not half a mile from Frank.

14.25: Helen was lying on the bed writhing and crying with pain in her left lower abdomen, constantly flexing her left hip in an attempt to reduce the pain – and Helen is no softie. She was very tender to pressure over the left lower abdomen, and the pain did seem to be confined to the abdominal cavity, and therefore probably originated from the organs contained within it. Despite my knowing Helen, taking the history of this present complaint, and examining her, I was still at a loss as to the cause of such pain. I gave her a muscle relaxant to try to reduce her immediate pain but it didn't help. There were several possible causes going through my mind. Problems with the ovary, but her period the week before had been normal and so it wasn't an ectopic pregnancy. Nor did it conform to the expectations of the excruciating pain caused by low distal left renal colic or kidney stone, and it didn't resemble any form of obstruction in her intestines. Finally I doubled back in my thinking: it might just be caused by a stone in the bottom part of her ureter, the tube between the kidney and the bladder. I was puzzled because the pain was so localised and didn't radiate. Could it be something to do with the psoas muscle, one of the muscles which controls the movement of the hip, because of the way she was flexing her thigh? Perhaps something unusual like a psoas abscess – but she had no fever. I had no choice but to send her in to Airedale for them to try to sort it out. Sometimes these cases clear up without further treatment if something, like a small ovarian cyst, has become twisted and then untwists when the body relaxes with pain-killing drugs.

14.50: Mr Ansley, a farmer out Lawkland way, phoned to say he had forgotten to collect his heart tablets and could he come and pick them up. I told him I would be at the surgery at 15.15 if he came along then, and advised him to read St Matthew Chapter 25.

15.15: I opened up the surgery in keeping with Scottie's pre-phoned arrangement in order to see a small lad who was up in the Dales on a school camping holiday. He had got a spell, as we call splinters in Yorkshire, stuck right up under his thumbnail from splitting reeds. A quick distraction of the boy's attention and there lay the spell in the forcep blades. He took it back to camp to show his mates.

Then my farmer friend arrived to pick up his heart tablets. I gave him a copy of our yellow practice leaflet in which our surgery hours are detailed, and checked that he had a Bible at home.

15.25: Annie phoned to ask if I'd come and see her husband Leonard. A few weeks back I had sent him in to Airedale at four o'clock in the morning when he suffered from crescendo angina. When I got to his house today he was extraordinarily anxious. This was nothing to do with his angina, but a severe anxiety attack to a level which is unusual to see. He had become worried by the fact that he was anxious, which was beginning to turn into a vicious circle. He really was in one hell of a state, and yet he had the insight to realise this, and knew that he was causing his wife trouble and distress.

Throughout all this he retained the dignity I remembered so well of him when he taught me PT at Giggleswick School, and he kept apologising as he had done the night I sent him in. I gave him some diazepam to help him ease down, and told Annie I'd call in again later that evening.

15.50: I was just leaving home to see John Coltman, who suffers from left ventricular heart failure and who had phoned to say he was having problems breathing, when a red Citroen pulled into our drive. Out of it got three walkers in their late fifties who explained they had just successfully completed the Three Peaks walk for the first time, taking ten hours to do it. Full marks to them; they must have risen early.

Ironically, however, as they returned to the sanctuary of their car one of the party, a fifty-nine-year-old woman, had fallen and received a bad gash on her chin which needed stitches. Scottie escorted her through the paddock to the surgery, taking the cordless phone with her. She would get the patient ready for stitching while I nipped off to see if I could fettle old John Coltman and his breathlessness.

15.55: I relieved John's left sided heart failure with an injection of diuretic which relieves the tension or pressure on the circulation and heart. The chronic bronchial constriction of his chest was eased with a second injection which dilated the bronchial tubes.

16.00:   I returned to the chin of our stalwart fell walker Mrs Woodbridge and stitched it. What she didn't know was that the chin injury was the least of her worries. She also had a Colles' fracture to her wrist, so I sent her off to Airedale Hospital for X-ray and forearm plaster.

16.30:   The kettle had just got on to the Aga when Harden Ward at Castleberg Hospital phoned to say Molly Robinson wasn't well. Molly had fallen at home some three weeks ago and fractured not the usual femur but her posterior pelvis. Also Magdelene Ayres wasn't too good, though I knew she'd be smartly dressed even so. Anyhow we got our cup of tea in and off I drove over the river to Giggleswick and the newly opened Harden Ward. The place only accepted its first residents last Wednesday, when Harden Bridge, the old isolation hospital, closed. Castleberg is much more convenient for us since it's only two minutes down the road, compared to the twelve minutes it took us to get to Harden.

I was looking for chest infections particularly, but neither of these two ladies had one, so I said we'd get urine specimens and send them to the laboratory on Monday. As I entered the ward I couldn't help but smile to myself as I caught sight of Magdelene checking her hair in a little hand mirror.

On the way home I called in to see if the cream had worked the oracle on Frank's extremity. It hadn't done as much as I had hoped, and my attempt at reduction failed. Frank accepted the pain stoically, and I had no option but to admit him to Airedale, where they would try icepacks followed by reduction and perhaps elective surgery later. A minute after I'd given up trying to manipulate his problem he was back on form. As we went downstairs he was laughing about beating me in a race if I gave him 10 yards' start. I thought I was being very discreet by sitting him down with his wife in the kitchen and closing the door as I used their hall phone to call the hospital. Obviously I wasn't. As I gave his age to the doctor, he came running out to say he wasn't seventy-six but seventy-eight, with a wink and a mischievous grin.

17.00:   I was just about to phone the police to ask them to accompany me to Lucy Wilson's, when Scottie took a message from the neighbour to say the home help had arrived with a key and they had discovered her upstairs, unconscious on the floor in her bedroom.

One hand on her cheek and one attempted movement of her arm told me that Lucy had been dead for about ten or twelve hours, since she was stiff with rigor mortis.

Although I've known her since I came to Settle and she'd been under my care for nearly as long, I had no idea as to the precise cause of her death. My duty therefore was to report the matter to the police as a sudden death. On my way out of the house I saw Lucy's elderly next door neighbour looking out and thought I ought to break the news to her. She's an old lady of similar age and, obviously unaware of her neighbour's death, thought I had just come in for a chat with her. Before I could utter a word she launched into a detailed account of how she'd got on at her own hospital appointment yesterday. I listened to her story, and then gently told her about Lucy. She was obviously shaken by the news, having been chatting with Lucy the night before, and she confirmed that she had seemed very lively and normal at 9 o'clock the previous evening. (The subsequent post mortem disclosed that Lucy had died of a sudden and massive brain haemorrhage.)

17.40:   Brian Parsons had phoned while I was out at Lucy's to ask me to call and see his father, Joe. Brian and I were boys at Giggleswick School together, and I remember him because he was always so much brighter than me. Old Joe remembered my athletics and I preferred this memory to my academic perform-ances. This wonderful old man of eighty-eight has chronic leu-kaemia and we had a good talk during which Joe very rationally admitted that looking after himself was getting beyond him.

I told him I would get him into Harden Ward tomorrow, and from there would push hard to get him to Greenfoot old people's home. Once there he would have his own room with his own bits and pieces around him. I also feel that it's just the right place for Joe, who would have so much to give to such a place, as well as receiving the care that this great old man so richly deserves.

I called in at the police station on the way home to set things in motion about Lucy and formally to report her death to the coroner.

19.30:   Mrs Tiplady from down the road phoned to say her chest was 'playing up again'. I whipped down and did my best with her emphysematous lungs, which give rise to her extreme breath-lessness, whilst trying to avoid another course of steroids.

19.35:   The mother of the little lad Paul I'd seen earlier screaming with stomach pains, carried through the phone review as requested, informing Scottie that he had settled down fine, and was now playing happily with his sister.

19.45:   A call from the mother of little Craig. His uncle had been playing with him in their kitchen and had grabbed Craig's legs, accidentally making him fall back on to their stone kitchen floor, on which he had cracked his head. He'd gone to bed but had woken up twice and vomited, and understandably they were concerned. I must say it didn't sound so good, and certainly I'd need to see him at some stage of the evening. I told his mother I'd be along in about an hour – after a brief supper.

20.10:   With a glass of sherry in my hand I spoke to Mrs Graham. She wanted to ask me about her ninety-six-year-old aunt from Worthing who was staying with them. She had fallen in the bathroom, hitting her head, and although Mrs Graham thought she was unharmed, she felt she ought to speak to me about it. She described how Aunt was laughing about it now, saying she ought to put more water with it; so together we thought she sounded OK. I told her to ring me again if she was concerned. I made a note to go to them on Sunday morning just to see this remarkable old lady and put a hand on her head.

20.30:   Before I could go out the door to see Craig, his mother phoned to say he was better and there was no point in my calling. I still thought I'd like to see him; it's no good telling the coroner that, 'His mother seemed to think he was all right.' A subdural haematoma, which is a blood clot between the inside of the skull and the brain which puts pressure on the brain if it expands, can be a killer in anyone's skull. When I got to the house Stephen, the father, was up in the bedroom with Craig, having just come in from working out in the fields making silage all day – one of life's hard workers. Craig was sleeping but woke as I examined him. Confused by the sudden disturbance, he blinked as he tried to work out what was going on. I examined him gently, his pupils were equal and reacted to my torch light in the dark bedroom. There was no neck stiffness and no other signs of meningeal irritation. (The meninges are the membranes which line the skull and protect the brain.) Most reassuring was the mischievous little smile on his face which gradually enlarged as he shook off his sleepiness. All was well. Mum and dad smiled their relief and Stephen, tired out though he must have been, walked me out to the car.

21.30: A return visit to Leonard who had calmed down considerably. He produced a list of questions which very sensibly he had prepared for me. The first was, 'Can I have a small whisky?' To which I replied no, he could have a large one.

22.45: On the way back from a visit to Giggleswick School, to which I'd been called to see a nasty sprained ankle, I noticed the lights were still on in Barbara and John's house, so I called in. Barbara has just returned from hospital after some major surgery. Her recent history starts with her developing a myeloma, a form of cancer of the bones, which has been successfully treated for the last eighteen months. She was doing terribly well when suddenly she developed a cancer of her descending colon and she now has a colostomy after the removal of the tumour and her distal colon. Barbara and John have discussed the situation with the surgeon, so the purpose of my visit was to talk about it with them. I've known them for years and have great respect for them both, not least for the courage they've shown in their lives, coupled with a deep, true Christianity.

I first got to know them just after I'd arrived in Settle during the vicious winter of 1962/63. They desperately wanted children, and had one son, William. Barbara subsequently suffered two late miscarriages. William was seventeen and working in a garage when he had a fatal car accident. John and Barbara decided to try for another child, though by then Barbara was in her late thirties. She succeeded in getting pregnant, but suffered another miscarriage. Yet again she became pregnant, and only in the last few weeks of this pregnancy were they robbed of their child. Determined not to give up they adopted two children, a boy and a girl, who are now both in their teens. Now she has this new problem.

Barbara is remarkably courageous, and still hasn't lost her spiritual strength. We sat and talked about all sorts of things including her pen and ink drawings which hang on the wall. She smiled as she recalled how fifteen years ago she had decided to learn pottery and had gone along to a local evening class. A few minutes into the lesson they were all given paper and pencil which she thought was odd, hoping they weren't going to have to draw their proposed designs. It turned out that she had gone into the drawing class by mistake, but, as with so many other things in her life, once she'd started she determined to carry on.

John poured us a dram and asked me if I recalled the time when I'd conned him into acting as my bodyguard. They used to farm out at Studfold and occasionally I called in on them when I was going home from a late night call, and we'd have a talk and a dram. One evening I stopped there on my way out to a call, and asked him if he'd like to come for the ride. John took great pleasure in reminding me that I hadn't got round to telling him the real reason behind my invitation until we were sitting outside the patient's house. The man had got a bit manic and become violent. I told John that if he heard me shouting he was to come in and sit on the chap, and then I jumped out of the car before he could demur. John recalled that his assistance wasn't required.

All I did last night with John and Barbara was to reinforce the fact that I was around and make sure they knew they could call me whenever they felt the need.

SUNDAY 10 JUNE

LUCKILY NO CALLS during the night. I reckon if I can sleep between midnight and 6 o'clock I'm OK the next day. Calls up to 2 a.m. and after 5 a.m. aren't too bad. Between 2 and 5 o'clock is bad, and 3.30 a.m. is the bottom. Having said this, I enjoy my night calls, and we very seldom get an irresponsible one. Just after breakfast it all started again. I took three phone review calls at 08.30, and in each case the problem either had resolved or was resolving. I find these 'phone reviews' invaluable. The patient knows that at a specific time in the near future their problem is going to be assessed, and this reassures them. The doctor knows that he will receive a progress report about the patient, and this will enable him to move the treatment in any direction, either by arranging further assessment by phone or by seeing the patient again as he thinks appropriate. It also enables the doctor to evaluate the success or failure of his advice or treatment.

09.00:   Mrs Baker phoned to say that she had a vicious face and head ache on the right side. From her description I thought it was trigeminal neuralgia, or tic douloureux as it is sometimes called. It's a peculiar and terrible pain associated with the fifth cranial nerve as it emerges through the small hole in the base of skull. If that nerve swells it becomes irritated and inflamed which then puts pressure on it and causes a terrible searing sort of pain. I believe it is excruciating, but thankfully I've never experienced it. I'd seen Mrs Baker in the surgery during the week and had given her a drug which is designed to inhibit the pain stimuli, in the hope of stopping the irritation. We discussed her pain and arranged her medication, and I asked her to phone-review at 12.30 that morning.

09.30 a.m.:   John rang to say he had another chest pain. I let him tell me about it, wondering whether I should be preparing to grab the defibrillator and ECG machine. We talked for a bit and it became clear that it was musculo-skeletal pain, because it occurred when he moved and heaved his chest. He then said that actually it wasn't too bad, and he wasn't worried but his wife had made him ring up. I was content to leave it there, but told him to get in touch again if he wasn't happy.

10.10 a.m.:   I had arranged a Sunday mini-surgery for 10.15 from the telephone requests already in, so I had to dash up the road to Mrs Bacon in response to her request for a visit before opening the surgery. The widow of the last vicar of Horton was in awful pain from acute lumbago. I gave her an injection of an anti-inflammatory drug which I know works well because I've used it myself.

10.20 a.m.:   Five minutes late for the impromptu surgery, I apologised to my four patients, briefly explaining the reason.

The first poor man, Tony, struggled into my examination room grunting with pain. He'd recently come off his motorbike on the Isle of Man for the second time. Five years ago he badly broke his arm. This year in a nasty spill he'd managed to break five ribs. Tony was unable to breathe without great pain, and he's been breathing shallowly to try and reduce the pain. As a result he's accumulated a lot of goo and muck in his lungs, but can't bear to cough to bring it up. Occasionally his cough reflex triggered and sent him on a brief journey through hell, from which he would emerge sweating and pleading for relief. It is difficult to resolve this cycle of events. Muscle relaxants, analgesics, antibiotics and bronchial dilators all have their place, as, later, do physiotherapists. You can't splint fractured ribs, for to live one must breathe, and to breathe one must move the rib-cage.

My remaining three cases were a middle ear infection; a rash of unknown origin, at least so far as the patient and I were concerned; and a scleral haemorrhage with normal blood pressure. This last patient received a rather hasty explanation of her lesion, with little time to ask her if she understood my account. The sclera is the white of the eye, and scleral haemorrhages are often dramatic and alarming since it's only when the patient looks at his or her eye in the mirror and sees blood redness where they previously possessed a shining white sclera that they become aware of the problem. Or alternatively someone says, 'Oh my goodness, what have you done to your eye?' A firm explanation and a comparison to small bruises in the skin usually reassures the patient and enables me to prescribe one of my favourite treatments: masterly inactivity, or more simply and literally, leave the bloody thing alone! On this occasion I asked the patient to use the phone-in at half past eight in two days' time, or before if she was worried.

10.50:   At this point in the affairs of Sunday morning the Church bells and the phone sounded simultaneously, but the summons of the latter was much stronger because Sheila, the matron at Giggleswick School, was on the phone to tell me that one of the boys, James Finch, had suffered a nasty accident to his foot. The detail was enough for me to buzz Scottie at home, ask her to come across and do the dispensing of pills for Tony and the middle ear whilst I hightailed it to the school surgery, leaving the scleral haemorrhage putting her coat on in my examination room.

When I arrived I found James lying on the couch in the school surgery's treatment room. The exposed top and side of his left big toe gaped at me from a nasty rotational tear wound. He'd apparently caught his foot in some rocks and the end of his big toe had been ripped away. He was in considerable pain but doing well to control his anxiety.

It's important to talk carefully and directly to patients at these junctures. By directly I mean physically close to and with eye contact. I reassured him as I worked that in a couple of months' time all would be OK and that such injuries to fingers and toes can heal amazingly well, although understandably James didn't seem too convinced by my reassurances as he lay there. I next completed the removal of the nail, already partly avulsed, and simply bound the flesh around the exposed bone. The thing concerning me most was the apparent degree of skin loss, for I thought a graft would probably be needed. I refrained from giving James any drugs immediately because he was coping so well. Often with a fairly serious wound like this the body shuts itself down for a while around the damaged area and the pain felt seems disproportionately small to the trauma. I asked the lads in the ambulance to give James a whiff of Entonox if they thought he needed it. This is a useful analgesic which is effective, but quickly disperses.

Elizabeth, the school padre's wife, went down with James, as I phoned his parents to explain what had happened. We were lucky to find them at home, and in this country. Things can be less easy if parents live in Vanuatu or Papua New Guinea as some of our parents do. Both James's parents are doctors and were able to assimilate the facts quickly.

James was taken to theatre later in the morning and the toe was repaired and skin grafted. The human body never ceases to amaze me, and particularly the manner in which the most mangled fingers resolve their traumatic deformities and take up near normal function. I sometimes tell my patients this to reassure them.

12.30: Mrs Baker telephoned on schedule to say that her right face pain was much better, so this appeared to prove that the diagnosis of tic douloureux was correct.

12.50:   Three calls came in from the Hellifield area. A patient wanting an injection; a lady suffering from terrible abdominal cramps; and Audrey Hogg to say that Frank was not so good today. This last was the most important. Audrey explained he hadn't been able to eat much lunch and his breathing and coughing were getting worse.

13.00:   Ten minutes later I let myself into Barton House Farm and found Audrey and her daughter Fiona looking anxious. The reason for their anxiety was obvious enough when I looked at Frank. He looked ill, dehydrated and depressed. He was unable to eat and had the greatest difficulty swallowing. I had to discuss with them all his admission to hospital, but first I wanted to talk to the Senior House Officer at Airedale to brief him about this difficult case. So I went on to Hellifield to deal with the other two patients and use the phone at the branch surgery in the village.

So to the thirty-year-old lady with the severe abdominal pains. When I arrived her brother was sitting on a stool outside the back door, basking in the sun and reading the *News of the World*. Without looking up he said 'She's upstairs.' Inside the house her father greeted me.

'I tried to phone, 'cause she's better now, Doc.' This was kind of him, and anyhow I like patients who get spontaneously better, and this I told him to save his embarrassment. Nevertheless I said I'd have a quick look 'just to make sure'.

He was right, she was still in bed but better from her menstrual pain, which had obviously been severe. I said cheerio as I left to the man on the stool, who continued to read his paper.

Last call was to give the injection to the lady who was very grateful because she thought I'd turned out on a Sunday just to see her. I didn't disenlighten her; there was no point, and she felt better with her assumption.

In the deserted surgery I phoned the hospital, and advised them about Frank Hogg. We discussed his admission for further assessment by the gastro-enterologist, Dr Gwyn Morgan.

Opposite: Audrey: 'We want to keep him
at home, Barry.'

Overleaf: Frank

I suddenly felt odd, and realised that my blood sugar was low. It was now reaching two o'clock and Sunday lunch would be waiting. I hate rushing meals, but Scottie had laid on another mini surgery at 2.30 p.m., assuming that at least I'd return home by 1.30.

14.30:   A urinary tract infection in a young lady. The symptoms were definite enough – frequency of urination, and pain on doing so – so I gave her an appropriate antibiotic to start forthwith and asked her to bring in a sample three days after the completion of the course of treatment. In this way we would not discover which particular wily organism had invaded her urinary tract, but she would be relieved of her distressing symptoms quickly, and hopefully we would later know that she was clear of infection.

A second middle ear infection in a girl of six years, and a phone call from a nurse I'd met the previous week and who had recovered from a virus infection only for her daughter to catch it. So I left some Calpol out for her, trusting her ability to cope with the problem. She sounded competent and was in the trade.

15.35:   Mark Nixon hobbled in with a distressing lumbago, of acute onset. An injection of an anti-inflammatory drug with a course of tablets to follow and some advice on rest and lifting took about fifteen minutes, and as I walked home at 15.50 Hilary, the assistant school matron at Giggleswick School, rang just to let me know that she had admitted another boy to the sanatorium with something fairly minor and was able to cope with it. She also wanted to discuss another pupil from Nairobi who we're a bit concerned about, because she may possibly have some tropical disease. It's not malaria; that's been ruled out. I've seen her Granny who lives locally and who tells me that the girl is worried about her boyfriend back home in Nairobi, which may be a contributory factor. However, the blood tests show an eosinophilia. These cells increase in number if you have an allergy, or the patient is hosting parasites. So we're on the lookout for possible causes such as bilharzia or even tic fever which I don't know a lot about. Bilharzia is the main candidate, and quite treatable these days. Another possibility is that it might be the remnants of glandular fever, the kissing disease which is common in the young, although previous tests have been negative for this.

16.00: Another nurse, this time from the medical ward at Aire-dale, came in not feeling so good, with aches and pains. I was just about to examine her when Scottie rushed in. She told me to get to Eric Bibby quickly – his wife had called to say that he had collapsed. I dashed off and I'm afraid lost track of the nurse, but Scottie had a chat and dealt with her.

On the way I had a sudden panic as I remembered that there are two brothers Eric and Allen, and they live in opposite directions. But I was sure it was Eric, because I remembered hearing 'opposite The Black Horse pub' mentioned, so I was speeding in the correct direction. As I pulled up at the house I saw Frank Knowles, Eric's brother-in-law, dashing in ahead of me and I followed him. I ran in to find Joan clinging to her husband's neck, sobbing. Things didn't look good and I'm sure she knew he was dead.

The first task was to detach her from him sensitively, but as quickly as possible and get her into the next room before I could attempt resuscitation. Having whisked Joan next door I got Frank to help me move Eric on to the floor and I started resusci-tation. Even as I was going through all the motions I could see he was clearly dead and had been for some minutes. It's infor-mation you take in intuitively as you're applying the practical physical actions. His pupils were widely dilated and there was no sign of life.

The figure of three minutes from the moment the heart stops is usually quoted as a maximum time that the cerebral tissue can be deprived of circulating blood. If resuscitation isn't started before then, there's little hope of reviving the patient. At a guess it was at least six minutes since what I was sure was a massive coronary had occurred, so I knew I was pretty well out of time. It is always a difficult and fraught few minutes, and the decision to cease resuscitation is never easy.

The problem then was that Eric was lying in the only pass-ageway through the house so we would have to move him.

I had asked Scottie to order an ambulance as I ran from the surgery, and the crew quickly arrived. I had to ask Joan if she wished me to have Eric's body taken to the chapel of rest. Unhap-pily I was compelled by these circumstances to rush this question upon her.

I felt very flat and inadequate. People hope somehow you

can work a miracle – put in a needle or shock the body with a defibrillator or whatever, somehow bringing the patient back to life. Inevitably you feel that pressure, and the inadequacy of not being able to do anything, heightened for me by the image of Joan so physically attached to the body when I arrived. This sort of sudden death is fairly numbing for everyone concerned, not least the doctor. I've known Joan and Eric and their two daughters for a long time, and nursed Joan's father for many years before he died. He was a great old character whose favourite phrase to me was, 'I want rubbin' out and makin' agen!'

I felt upset and shocked by Eric's death. Just three days ago returning from school surgery I'd seen him and pulled in to pass the time of day. He was on cracking form, and now his body lay before me dead. It was unexpected, so sudden, a violence within me.

17.00: I got home and sucked deeply through the slice of lemon in my well sugared Earl Grey. The CD throbbed with Beecham's 2nd Sibelius. Helped by the music, I tried to ease my upset at Eric's death. But then the phone rang again.

17.30: Another set of calls to the south-east of our patch. Douglas, the chef from the Black Horse pub in Hellifield, phoned to say he had severe lumbago and was rigged in bed like a sheep on its back. Seven miles and eight minutes down the road found me back in Hellifield and I eventually reached the chef. Why is it that visiting hotel staff is nearly always such a catacombic adventure through passages and odd shaped storeroom spaces? Douglas didn't seem to have too much spasm, not as much as I've seen in many people with lumbago, but it was his first episode and I treated him appropriately. They had dinner for forty people in three hours' time so his second chef was in at the deep end.

18.05: Just as I was walking back out through the hotel's kitchens Scottie phoned to say Frank Hogg was bad, so I drove back to see him. His condition confirmed my decision to admit him. I couldn't help but reflect that I'd given Airedale Hospital a lot of custom this weekend.

18.40: When I phoned home again from the farm to check for any other calls Scottie told me Mr Bower from Long Preston had rung to say his wife was having difficulty breathing, so I called in on my way home and was able to help her heart failure a little, but she seemed very ill, and I talked to her husband to make sure that he realised how ill she was. She is John Lewis's patient and he would see her next morning. It proved the worth of phoning home before driving back and thereby fed my obsession with communication.

19.10: Just by the road between Long Preston and Settle lies Skirbeck Farm. I always regard the long sloping pasture which leads down the hill to the farm with delight. It somehow epitomises good farming, and on Robin's land you'll never see a gap in a wall; the gates always hang well; and the yard is always somehow just swept clean. Mary, his wife, died last year and Robin himself is just home from hospital after a slight stroke. In passing I called to see how he was, and we chatted for a while, walking through the yard to the accompanying barks of his five sheepdogs. He's a little slower, drags his left leg a fraction, struggles for the occasional word, but he will without doubt continue to farm at Skirbeck.

19.40: Home to the phone ringing about little Christopher who had a balanitis, an infected swelling of the end of his penis. Mum had some appropriate cream in the house, so I told her to wash him and explained how to apply it, telling her to ring me again if she wanted me to see him during the evening, and anyway to phone her own doctor, Eric Ward, during tomorrow's phone-in.

20.00: The yard arm was well down and I felt a G&T and some more Sibelius would be a fair contribution to precede supper. I thought about my garden, my broad beans, the weeds, that bloody convolvulus I'd spotted this weekend and the tomatoes in my greenhouse which have already embarked upon their usual survival course.

21.00: Supper with Scottie was undisturbed and at 21.30, just as I was setting off to see Joan Bibby, she herself phoned to say that she was all right. 'I've a cup of Horlicks in front of me and I'm off to bed.' Although her brother was there, both her daughters are away, one teaching in Germany, the other away camping in the Loire valley. Joan told me they'd already managed to track down the camp site and find the daughter in France via Colin Smith, a local chap who amazingly was able to recognise the site from her description, and find a phone number in his files.

I'll have to sort out the necessary death certificate tomorrow. I'd seen Eric the other day, and I'm sure the cause of death was a coronary thrombosis, so there won't be any need for a post-mortem.

23.00 Mrs Tiplady phoned to say that her daughter and boy-friend had just returned from a day out having had an accident on their way home and pranged the van, and now the boyfriend was lying on the sofa in their front room and he seemed very dopey. When I arrived he stayed slumped in the chair, attended by girlfriend and Mrs Tiplady. I asked if they would kindly leave us for a moment so I could make my examination more freely. There didn't seem to be any signs of concussion, and I had a suspicion that more of the problem stemmed from his worry about the damaged van. He was staying the night so I gave the usual advice about head injuries, asking them to ring me if he vomited or had bad headaches, or they were otherwise concerned. I then returned to the surgery to complete some of the day's paperwork.

WE SLEPT WELL last night, a second night with no calls between midnight and six o'clock was a bonus. From habit we wake at 06.50; I love breakfast and early mornings. I was just settling down to ten minutes with the paper rather thinking that my weekend was over, and just revving up for Monday morning's phone-in at 08.30 when that machine rang yet again.

Mrs Steele didn't have to say much for me to know that George was having another coronary thrombosis. Scottie phoned for an emergency ambulance for the fourth time in forty-eight hours as I scrambled the car down the road to Northfields and George. He marked my peremptory entry into his bedroom with a grunt of 'Sorry, Doc.' He was sweating, pale and ill. I examined him briefly. His blood pressure was down, but his heart rhythm, for George, not too bad. I administered my usual cocktail of Diamorphine and Stemetil, and asked the lads who by this time

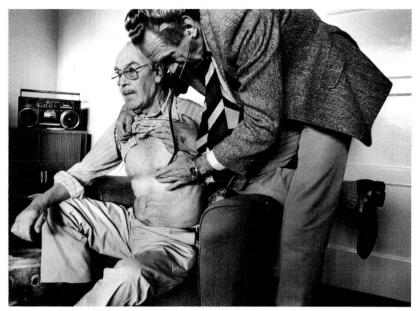

George, back home

had arrived with a chair stretcher to manoeuvre him so that he stayed flat, and not to elevate his head because that might compromise the circulation to his brain. Then a note for the ambulance driver, written quickly whilst weighing up the pros and cons for accompanying George to hospital. I decided against this, partly based on the fact that this particular likeable old bugger will probably see me out anyway. Off he went to Intensive Care, blue lights flashing and all. I returned to the bungalow to talk to his wife, and left a few minutes later with two lovely trout taken by George the day before from the river just 50 yards from his home.

I said good morning to the girls as I walked through reception, apologised to Barbara, our practice manager, for being five minutes late for the phone-in, and tied a knot in my handkerchief so that I wouldn't forget the trout in the back of the car.

'Any night calls, Barry?' asked David, our trainee.

'None after midnight,' I replied.

'Oh that's not so bad then.'

MY LAST PATIENT of this evening's surgery kindly drove me up the hill so I could go for a run in my favourite dale. As the noise of the car's exhaust receded it was replaced first by silence, then by wonderful music – curlews. The call of this graceful bird is the most haunting of all for me, and their gliding flight an aerodynamic beauty. Mrs Jimmy Clay and I were once discussing this beauty with the Colonel sitting across from us twitching with impatience because he wasn't interested, and wanted to talk about fishing. Jimmy told me that there was a local legend that if the curlew ever disappeared from this particular dale the world would come to an end. I am always therefore particularly glad to hear them whenever I go there.

Running along the bottom of the dale I passed the spot where over the years I've buried my three dogs, the last being only four months ago. Foss had gone off his legs, and after a night sitting with him by the Aga we had to call again on Keith Bolger, the vet, who had so sympathetically and kindly put down my other two dogs. With Foss's passing, contact with one of my more eccentric patients also became one more step removed.

George Staveley could be a difficult customer – he might shout and bawl, and occasionally become a little depressed – but for those who understood him the excesses of this old character were acceptable, and I for one shared many laughs and evenings with him.

He was the seventh son of the keeper for the Gearstones grouse moor, part of the Farrer estate, not far from the famous Ribblehead viaduct. In 1926, when he was in his twenties, George decided to emigrate to Canada, with his sheepdog Spring, but without his lady friend Dorothy. Leaving Dorothy behind was, he sometimes admitted to me, the only big mistake in his life.

'I should'a taken her wi' me!' There was no bitterness in this admission but a deep and hidden sadness.

For five hard and lonely years George worked on the grain trains and in mining, living a frugal life, and sending all his money back to Dorothy. He returned from Canada into the slump of 1931, bringing Spring with him even though her journey and quarantine cost £100. 'I'd never a' left her,' he'd say to me.

The first time I examined George's belly I discovered a huge surgical scar to the right side, and realised he'd been lucky to return from Canada himself. He recounted that he 'got a helluva pain in me belly, right down here. Ee, I was badly. Whitey, the chap I shared with, put a pile of plates on top of the old stove till they got nice and hot, then he'd pass one to me every so often to put on me belly, and by God the warmth did relieve the pain.'

I thought of his appendix abscess cooking away to its critical conclusion of peritonitis, masked by the temporary easing of pain; then the abscess bursting into his abdominal cavity; followed by a two day journey on a flat cart with his comrade Whitey driving on the horses towards Calgary hospital. The surgeon did well that day. The big scar bore witness to the large incision he needed to see into George's abdomen during surgery.

George and Dorothy were married and bought Fourdale Farm with the money he had religiously sent home from Canada. Dorothy became pregnant three times, but never reared a child. The only baby actually born lived a few hours, but the little boy was dead when Dr Lovet arrived in pony and trap having galloped across Swarthmoor from Austwick village 5 miles to the south-west. 'He gev him to me and we wrapped him in some newspaper, and I went out and buried him,' George told me once, pausing to take a puff on his pipe. 'And I know to within an inch of where he's buried, but nobody else does.' And now nobody ever will. I sometimes ponder what a man that boy might have been.

Fifteen years ago one November morning Meg, an eight-year-old fourth generation descendant of George's well-travelled companion Spring, gave birth to two pups. He drowned one just before I got there on my rounds, and I cussed him for it. The remaining pup he called Foss after Stainforth Foss the water force on the River Ribble close by his village. At much the same time I regretfully concluded that George had a gut cancer, and six months later when he was unable to cope any longer with Foss I bought him off George for £15. There would never have been any question of giving him away.

Foss was a year old by the time George died. After the death of this fascinating man, I regretted not having spent more time listening to his tales. On the odd evenings when I did go up to see him I'd invariably take a bottle of Scotch with me and sometimes a tape recorder, which I wish now I'd taken every time. We'd discuss his years in Canada, grouse, his hero Harry Lauder, and sheep. George's life was sheep and he knew an awful lot about them and would talk with such infectious enthusiasm about the creatures that even the uninitiated like me became drawn in.

When I'm on a long car journey I play the cassettes of our conversations, and enjoy the tales told in his rich, sometimes incomprehensible, Dales accent. Each airing reveals another phrase or word not previously noticed.

In his youth at Ribblehead he courted a girl who lived in Dent, 8 miles away. One way to get there was the long walk over the fell, but George preferred a shorter way, under the fell by way of the Blaemore railway tunnel. All one and a half pitch black miles of it.

'But wasn't it difficult in the dark, George?' I asked in amazement.

'Oh no,' George replied. 'I had a stick and I just walked on the line. One, two, three, tap. One, two, three, tap. It was easy enough once you got the rhythm.' George used to set off on his philanderings after tea so I asked incredulously if he came back that same evening.

'Oh yes, I had to get back. Get my arse kicked if I didn't!'

I started to picture the treacherous journey and the ever-present threat from along the tracks.

'But what about trains? It must have been a bit dangerous.'

'No, no,' came the pipe-sucking reply, 'you'd feel a great puff o' wind from in front or behind as the train came whichever way, and you just got to the other side. No, no, it were safe enough.'

'What if there were two trains?' I asked tentatively.

'Oh, didn't often 'appen, but then you'd get the puffs of wind and then a terrible sort of still, and you nipped into one of them there burrow holes in the side of the tunnel.' I tried to imagine how the young Romeo would have appeared to his Juliet after this walk in the days of steam. The guy in the advert for Black Magic had absolutely nothing on George.

FOUR MONTHS AGO, some thirteen years after my last evening of storytelling with George, I buried my last living contact with him, my companion Foss, up in the dale alongside my other two dogs.

IT WAS FIVE DAYS since I'd seen Willie Morphet out at Wigglesworth Hall, and then he'd been in his bed and not that keen to move out of it. I'd heard on the grapevine that he was more active and had even been to Thorpes the newsagents to get his papers, which meant he must have driven there in the Landrover. After Willie had clouted a wall in March I'd had a talk with him and grounded him, 'No driving on tarmacadam,' I'd told him, leaving him free to drive round his land if he must. Advice he'd obviously ignored. All things considered I thought it was time to drive out and see how the old devil was doing.

With the roof down, I motored out through Rathmell village. The countryside was as dramatic as ever, with the stark yellow rectangles of silo-cut fields in the distance contrasting with the vivid green swathes of grass in the fields which had been cut, but not yet gathered in. Rain had fallen on some of the cut grass yesterday and this, Willie's neighbour John Booth had told me, would never be good quality and will be relegated to winter feeding for store cattle.

I expected to find Willie in bed at Wig Hall, and was surprised to find his front room empty of life, the only inhabitant being an unwatched television set broadcasting the cricket. I wandered around the side of the farm where I found a truck and trailer. This belonged to another branch of the Booth family who live a few miles away from Wiggleworth. Then I noticed a sheep emerge from the old barn at the back of Willie's house. Like the surrounding fields, the animal was shorn. I wandered into the barn to be greeted by a pair of striped Winceyette pyjamas in an old dressing gown, shambling about with a tin of red paint and a stick. Once my eyes had become accustomed to the gloom I could see the pyjamas contained Willie in full command, giving orders to the Booths as the last of his twenty sheep were clipped. Willie is not one to miss his own sheep being sheared and was there to supervise the event and, most importantly, dab them with the red marker which proclaimed his continued ownership.

Robert Booth wielded the electric shears while the whole Booth tribe helped. Anne, Robert's wife, was rolling up the fleece, rather a grand description for some of the moth-eaten articles of which Willie's wizened animals had been relieved. The children were all playing their roles. One hung on to the safety switch,

poised to cut the power to the shears at the first sign of trouble; the others shepherded the creatures one by one from the pen into the barber's seat in the other half of the barn, and swept the floor in between each customer. I asked the age of the beast being given the treatment as I entered, and Robert replied that he wasn't sure but he thought Willie would soon have to give it its twenty-first birthday party.

Willie looked fit and was certainly enjoying himself, complaining that things weren't being done to his satisfaction. I stood, bag in hand, soaking in the scene for a few moments until Anne was struck by a thought.

'Can you have a look at Nicholas, Doctor?'

The youngest of the clan was herded across to me in the corner of the cobweb-ridden impromptu surgery. The lad has had a history of febrile convulsions and today he felt warm so it was certainly worth treating him quickly to alleviate any possible causes of fever. Looking down his throat I could see he had a nasty tonsillitis, so I went out to the car to get him some sachets of antibiotic, and Anne put them in her pocket and completed folding the fleece.

Having examined my unexpected extra patient there was nothing I could do but wait for the agricultural job to be completed. Willie certainly wasn't moving from that barn until the last sheep had been shorn.

Once the last geriatric animal had made its way into the field, Willie ambled back to the farmhouse, holding on to my arm for support. While he was getting himself a cup of tea I had a word with the Booths. They expressed concern that they'd found Willie driving the Landrover again when they'd arrived.

When I had grounded him a couple of months back after he'd started getting double vision I had hoped it would be the last we'd hear about it. Obviously not.

Back in the kitchen I examined Willie and was pleased to hear a clear chest, all signs of pneumonia gone; but knew I had to tackle the thorny subject of mobility.

'I hear you're driving again, Willie.'

A long silence while Willie decided upon a response. 'Aye,' was all I got.

'You mustn't drive on the road, you know that.'

'I'm all right. I'm going to get a new car anyhow.' I knew

that up until a year ago Willie had owned a large Mercedes, and I'd no reason to believe that the old beggar was going to change his style at this stage. I reinforced my point that he mustn't drive on tarmacadam, whatever.

'I can't promise that,' was the best I could elicit.

In the ensuing conversation he didn't say he would, nor did he say he wouldn't, but just repeated that he couldn't promise, just as though he didn't want to lie to me about it.

It's a real problem and one which may require some drastic action. I'll have to look up when he last came for his over-seventy medical and take it from there. Ninety-two would be a pretty good time to stop driving in anyone's book, but I fear it will be more of a struggle with this particular motorist.

As I was about to drive off some more Booths, Willie's neighbours Freda and John, walked around the corner looking, they explained, to see if they could put their sheep back in the field which had become the temporary sheep-shearing corral. Though clearly reluctant to inform on him they eventually reinforced my fears by confirming they'd seen him wandering all over the tracks in the Landrover. My worry is not so much what he does to himself, but what he might do to others in his path.

Back in the front room of the huge house Willie was totally exhausted from the efforts of his sheep management and it wasn't the time to try again with him. That will have to wait until another day.

Opposite: Willie

THIS MORNING I RECEIVED a letter from Dr Alan Darnborough, our consultant radiologist, which reads:

'As a result of shortage of cash, and, therefore, staff, we are closing Room 2. This will result in delay for some X-ray examinations.'

If things go on like this for much longer we'll be no better off than my friend Denis Lockhart was in Kenya thirty years ago.

Denis worked as a medical officer for the Colonial Medical Service, in the little village of Tambach which perches on the very edge of the Rift Valley some 300 miles north-west of Nairobi. I stopped off with him for a fortnight during the return leg of Pegasus Overland in 1960 in order to work with him. In that brief time I learnt a lot about simply getting on and managing with whatever medical kit was available.

In addition to travelling the reserve, Denis was responsible for the seventy-bed hospital in the village. On my third day there an old chap of seventy-six arrived after walking for three days to get to the hospital. He had a terrible injury, a slash from a penga bush knife which went right through his jawbone on the right side of his face. We operated on him, with Denis wielding the scalpel and me assisting, drilling the bone to get wires through in order to pull the fragments of the jawbone together. Halfway through the operation I couldn't help looking at the two of us in our gowns, masks and gloves and wondering if we were the same people who had been drinking at the Lincoln's Inn pub in Dublin not that long before. There we were in the heart of Africa, standing on either side of an operating table performing bone surgery in the most primitive conditions, and I remember thinking, 'Isn't life fantastic fun?'

The anaesthetic was administered by way of a mask on which you poured ether. This was done by the medical orderlies, who were extremely skilled and experienced with this primitive but easily available form of anaesthetic.

On this day, however, the patient was turning slightly blue, a sign of a lack of oxygen in the blood. 'How about a bit of oxygen, Denis?' I suggested.

Denis looked at the patient and then at Joseph, the medical orderly, and said, 'That's a damn good idea, isn't it, Joseph.'

They didn't say any more, and we continued operating. A

few minutes later nothing had happened, so I said again, 'Hey, what about that oxygen?'

Denis again turned to Joseph, 'That *is* a good idea. What do you think, Joseph?'

'It's a very good idea, *daktari*' (Swahili for doctor), replied Joseph, and gave a flashing smile so broad it was visible either side of his mask. I realised at last that there was a problem.

'Where is it then?' I said.

'About 40 miles away in Eldoret, and then there may not be any,' replied Denis, with a good-humoured chuckle.

You learn to fit in with the local possibilities and short-comings very quickly in a set-up where there is no choice but to get on with it. And thankfully in this case the patient, despite his seventy-plus years, was sitting up right as rain that evening, having a bowl of soup.

Denis lived in a bungalow from which we would emerge early each day and get into his Landrover. This was parked up a ramp adjoining the building and (for reasons I was yet to discover) Denis would take the handbrake off and let it roll backwards until it gained enough momentum to jump start the engine.

Then we had a drive down, down, down, to the base of the valley along terrible twisty roads, including one particularly hairy promontory known as Brighton Pier.

At the bottom of the valley we would spend the morning at the village of Tot. Denis ran a little clinic which was built on stilts to keep it safe from the ravages of insects and animals. We attended to the people's illnesses; operated, if necessary, and met all sorts of astonishing characters.

At the end of the day we would negotiate the tortuous climb back up another road to the top of the rift valley to attend another clinic. Then we'd travel back to Denis's quarters.

As he approached the bungalow, Denis would build up speed and shoot the Landrover up the little ramp, making it thump into the side of the building. This would wake the houseboy, who would come running up to the window just in time to catch the uncoiling flex which Denis threw deftly to him. This flex, connected to the Landrover battery, was for the moment left dangling through the window.

After a welcome shower, a few G&Ts and dinner, the houseboy would bring out a bottle of whisky and put it on the table. As darkness fell he would come back and screw a lightbulb into the socket on the end of the coil of flex from the Landrover. This would provide our illumination in the absence of any generator. We would sit there, sometimes on our own, other evenings with Denis's friends, enjoying a few well-earned drams and some good stories. As the night wore on the bulb would begin to dim. When it gave its last flicker we knew it was time for bed.

The next morning the bulb would be removed, the flex coiled up and thrown back into the Landrover. We'd leap aboard, let go the brake and the Landrover would trundle down the ramp. At the right moment Denis would let out the clutch and start the engine. The battery would be charged during the day's travels in time for the next evening's illumination

Once again I read the letter from Alan Darnborough which had arrived this morning. Shortages and closures. This must mean reduced care for my patients. I can't imagine we'll ever approach the primitive medical conditions I experienced in Tambach, but this latest closure is certainly a step in the wrong direction.

Whatever else, Alan's letter was the final straw for me. My revised letter of resignation from the Conservative Association went in the post today.

Opposite: Audrey and Fiona
Overleaf: John William Peter's christening

TUESDAY
11
DECEMBER

TODAY HAS BEEN a glorious but sad day. Glorious because this morning was one of brilliant sunshine with a crystal blue sky, when the limestone scars appeared to rip through the green mantle of the hills. Sad because during the night Willie Morphet slammed the door in the face of the Grim Reaper for the last time. A week ago Freda had found Willie sitting silent and immobile in front of his kitchen fire having suffered a stroke. He died last night at the age of ninety-three.

As the year, and therefore this diary, draw to a close, I am moved to reflect on the fortunes of the other people featured in its pages. Most have happily recovered to return to their daily tasks, with our involvement in their lives quite rightly dismissed. Bryn's latest brain scan was clear, a year after the removal of his tumour; ten-year-old Duncan's recovery is total after incredible and successful surgery to remove the angio-fibroma, a tumour which once invaded his facial bones. Isabel is about to receive her best Christmas present, a new left knee joint after the successful replacement of the right knee.

Other stories, however, have drawn to a close. Magdelene Ayres, who always dressed so immaculately, and that kindly old farmer Frank Beresford, both died on Harden Ward in our local community hospital, near to their families and old friends.

Audrey and Fiona Hogg still found time to welcome the whole filming team into their home during their loving care of Frank. 'Now put that camera away and I only want to see a glass in your hands!', she'd warned them as we sat around the fire in the sitting room of Barton House Farm. Across the hall, in the next room, Frank lay resting, aware of the warm hospitality his wife and daughter were providing. A week later he died peacefully at home of the cancer with which he had struggled for so long.

Soon after I had sat in the church full of flowers at Frank's funeral, I attended another ceremony at which the attention was turned upon a wee baby, John William Peter, whose godfather I then became. Just thirty years ago, in that same village, I had assisted at the birth of his uncle.

So when I look back at this year I must feel encouraged by my patients' successes, saddened by the friends I have lost, and heartened by the new lives which continue to enter our world. I suppose, all in all, it's been just another year.

10/1

Margaret Ross
Christmas '92